A GUIDE TO LIBRARY AND INFORMATION SCIENCE JOBS

A GUIDE TO
LIBRARY AND INFORMATION SCIENCE JOBS

Mahendra Kumar Seth

ABHIJEET PUBLICATIONS
DELHI-110 094

ABHIJEET PUBLICATIONS
2/46 Tukhmeerpur Extension
Delhi 110 094
Phone: 22181492, 55698474
e-mail: abhijeet_singh@vsnl.net
abhijeet_singh@indiatimes.com

A GUIDE TO LIBRARY AND INFORMATION SCIENCE JOBS

First Published 2006

ISBN 81-88683-92-2

PRINTED IN INDIA

Published by J.K. Singh for Abhijeet Publications, Delhi 110094, Lasertypeset by Rajesh Data Services, New Delhi and Printed at Himanshu Printers, Delhi.

Preface

This book is an attempt to create awareness on the secrets of interview success among the students and professionals in the field of Library & Information Science (LIS). The purpose is to meet the high demand of job seeking students/in-service candidates appearing various government, private and departmental interviews/competitive examinations in their respective fields. This is basically prepared for LIS professionals, with all types of questions and answers (Descriptive/Objective/Multiple Choice etc.) by reviewing various current interviews, examinations, suggestions from experts, specialist, etc.

It is also an attempt to present a comprehensive guide on current interview system for sure success especially in the various departmental interviews or fresh candidates. The work contain sufficient current and up-to-date sources presented/published in different current journals, magazines, seminar/conferences, discussions/forums, meetings, interview board, and Internet resources etc. related to Library and Information Science (LIS) and Information Technology (IT) fields. This book can be consulted by both the interviewed/interviewers/examiners/examined for a grand success of the same.

The entire book is having three different sections: i. descriptive information on interview, CV and LIS fields, ii. Objective and multiple questions & answers, iii. Selective LIS & IT resources. At the end an alphabetical glossary of words are provided for a ready reckoner for all possible questions in the field of LIS & IT. Each section is clear and unique in its area and easy to retain the answers in mind without any loss of memory. It is based on newly revised syllabus of SLET/NET and latest interviews methods adopted in the present digital libraries environment. It serves as a complete guide in the hand of the person who can succeed in all respects of his carrier in the field.

All attempts have been made by the author to make the work extremely comprehensive, exhaustive and complete so that candidates making use of the work must succeed in all respect. In the accomplishment of this work suggestions, assistance and guidance have been received from well-known authorities and interviewers of the related field. I am so thankful to all of them for their kind help and guidance. If this work could prove useful to the professionals, the author will feel amply rewarded. Any further suggestion for the improvement of the work will be given high importance for incorporating in the future edition.

Mahendra Kumar Seth

Contents

Preface v

SECTION I: LONG MULTIPLE TYPE Q/A

1. Library Automation 3
2. Electronic/Digital Library 9
3. Consortia in Libraries 13
4. Library Networking 18
5. World Wide Web/Internet 26
6. Library Vs. Internet 31
7. Reasons Why the Internet is No Substitute for a Library 33
8. Internet Search Tips and Strategies 37
9. TQM in Libraries 44
10. Marketing of Information Products and Services for Libraries 50
11. Marketing and Total Quality Management 55

SECTION II: OBJECTIVE/MULTIPLE TYPE QUESTIONS/ANSWERS

1. Information and Communication 63
2. Information and Reference Sources/Services 70

3. Information Processing and Organization/Retrieval 76

4. Management of Libraries/Information Centres 94

5. Information Technology 99

SECTION III: SHORT/OBJECTIVE TYPE FOR BOTH INTERVIEW/WRITTEN

1. Contribution of Prof. S.R. Ranganathan 127

2. Library Legislation in India 130

3. Important Library (Resources) Journals 131

4. List of Some Indian Library Journals & Place of Publications 135

5. Major Library Consortia and Organizations in the International basis 136

6. Library and Information Science Links 137

7. Library Software 139

8. Sci-Tech Databases 141

9. Indian Discussion Forums 145

10. Computer Capacity Measurement 146

11. Library Organizations/Associations 146

12. Word and their Origin 147

13. Library and Information Science Job Listing 148

14. Library Schemes of Classifications Origin (Year) 149

15. Universal Decimal Classification Quick References Table 150

SECTION I
(Long Multiple Type Q/A)

1

Library Automation

Library automation, which started in late 70s in few special libraries, has now reached most of the university libraries. It is yet to take off in college libraries in India owing to various problems. This paper tries to identify the barriers, analyze the convenient steps in automating the library and the technology available. Library automation means use of computer with network assistance in a library for the library function and other activities like house keeping operation such as acquisition, serial, cataloguing, and classification, etc and use of cdrom, internet, intranet and other advanced telecommunication system.

Definition: (i). The automatic handling of parts between progressive production processes. (ii). It is technology of automatic working in which is the handling methods.It includes mechanization of various process and their operations as well as the use of mechanics, equipments, tools, , i.e: all sort of mechanical device, automatic mechanics, electronic equipments and other systems.

Why Automation: Ranganathan 4th law is coming under this preview like save the time of readers.

(i) It improves control over vast collection of library

(ii) It control over the library house keeping operation like acquisition, serial , circulation and cataloguing modules, etc.

(iii) It control the sharing resources among the libraries (ex: union List or union catalogue)

(iv) Except this it relive the library staff from many clerical and administrative jobs in library.

Need

- ➢ It create efficient service in the library
- ➢ Provide correct and accurate service
- ➢ Control the literature explosion
- ➢ Operation by the multi - user
- ➢ Satisfying the users needs
- ➢ Resource sharing among the libraries for the common utilization and avoid duplication
- ➢ Be economical
- ➢ Save the time of the readers
- ➢ Retrieval of information very quick

Library automation means automatic technical processing in library like the house keeping operation and other advanced electronic media, like online technology, internet, intranet, cd - rom technology, etc. Automatic operation of the library function and activities, it called the library automation. Means the way of mechanical process. It is mainly control of library routine work.

Why library automation

Even though this question seems to be very fundamental it is essential to emphasize this aspect, as the library automation is yet to take off in majority of the Indian libraries. Secondly, while justifying need for library automation more than cost-effectiveness the benefits derived by the library users become the major consideration. Since library does not happen to be an economic entity such benefits need to be looked at in a different perspective. To appreciate the advantages it becomes necessary to highlight the different levels of library automation. For convenience it can be visualized at four levels:

1. Library cataloging system
2. House keeping operations and networking
3. Development of electronics/ CD-ROM library/ products
4. E-mail system and internet

The *library catalogue* or index to the collection forms the base for most of the library activities such as acquisition, reference, bibliographic service, inter-library loan etc. The users of library card catalogue will appreciate how fast is the retrieval, search and printing in automated environment. If the same system is available in network environment, users can have simultaneous access to the same database. From the library staff point of view the cumbersome job of printing the cards and their subsequent filing gets eliminated. Also, it conserves space and saves stationary.

The second level automation will be to use software which can handle all the *house keeping operations* of the library such as acquisition, circulation and serial control thus creating a network within the library or becoming part of the existing network of the institution. Networking of computers within an organization helps the users to browse the cataloguing system from any of the workstation/terminal.

A very handy technology available for library is the electronics/CD-ROM products which can be considered at the third level. The *development of electronics/CD-ROM collection* not only conserves space but also provides multi-user access in network environment. There are many self-tutorial CD-ROMS available with multi-media effect. Libraries facing high incidence of mutilation of materials will benefit from such electronic products. Also people doing empirical research can download data and directly take it to other software platform for analysis and making graphical presentation.

Other technology which libraries can make use of is the *e-mail* system. This not only reduces the recurring expenditure but also be effective and fast. Sending reminders for non-receipt of journals by e-mail has proved to be very cost-effective. In addition to this, sharing of resources among libraries become easy. Few public domain e-mail software are available and there will be no additional expenditure incurred.

Another technology which has revolutionized the information world is the development of internet. Subscribers of *Internet,* in addition to getting access to various public domain databases and services, will also get free e-mail and fax facility. Some publishers have started giving content pages of journals and libraries having subscription to such journals can also have full text of the articles. Many academic and research institutes have given free access to their working papers.

Pre-Requisites

There have been some pre-requisites for the execution and implementation of any project. Folloing are the basic requirements of library automation;-

1. Finance

2. Hardware
3. Library Maintence Software
4. Motivation of Library Staff
5. Willingness of the parent Organisation

Planning

1. Re - engineering the library process like: cost, quality, service, speed and better control.
2. Strengths (What the library currently does well).
3. Weakness (What the library current problems)
4. Opportunities (Forecasting future benefit of library services)

Hardware Aspect

1. Server
2. UPS
3. CVT
4. Nodes with LAN Card
5. Input Devices: Barcode Scanner - CCD, Scanner, Sign Pad and Data Collecting Unit (DCU)
6. Output Devices: Laser Printer/ Dot Matrix and Visual Display Unit (VDU)
7. Storage Technologies: Magnetic Media, Optical Storage (CD-ROM) and Data Cartridge

Software Aspect

1. System Software or Operating Software: UNIX, LINUX, WINDOWS NT, SQL etc.
2. Application Software: LIBSYS, ALICE for WINDOWS, VTLS, HORIZON etc.
3. Technical Aspect:

- Can the software perform the necessary functions in an appropriate time?
- Can the software able to run under the available hardware/ operating software?
- What are the data limits / size / quality.
- What communications protocols are supported?
- Capability for future expansion/ upgrading

Barriers of Library Automation

Following could be the few possible barriers of library automation:

- ➢ Fear of adverse impact on employment
- ➢ Apprehension that the technology could be too expensive
- ➢ The library staffs have to undergo extensive training.
- ➢ Lack of support from the management, may be owing to budget constraints
- ➢ Fifth reason could be retrospective conversion of data.

Let us examine each of the points. If we analyze the various jobs such as book acquisition, technical processing, circulation and reference service one can conclude that human interference is necessary at each and every step. The only area where substantial manpower can be saved is the cataloguing. The data entered at the time of ordering can be used for cataloging with some updating would eliminate multiple card preparation and subsequent filing. The manpower thus saved can be utilized in retrospective conversion and later on for analytical cataloguing or introducing new services. Therefore, there will be no adverse impact on employment.

There is an apprehension that the technology, both hardware and software would be expensive and unaffordable. The cost of hardware and software depends on the level of automation. From the user point of view cataloguing system is most important and also forms the base for other library activities. Keeping these two points in view UNESCO developed a PC based software titled 'CDS/ISIS' and is available at a very nominal price to all the libraries in developing countries. For details librarians may contact ATIRA/NISSAT.

This software which works on a simple IBM compatible PC/XT is also available on UNIX and NOVELL platform. Recently the WINDOWS version has also been released. This software can export data in ISO 2709 format and therefore at later stage if one decides to go in for some other software, data transfer poses no problem. INFLIBNET has developed a public domain library software titled 'ILMS' which is available on DOS AND UNIX platform. With the recent government policy the PCs and other accessories have become affordable. The cost of different hardware has been listed in the annexure I.

The in-house training for handling the software is usually provided by the developers and one can choose the software which can suit their budget. However, training for CDS/ISIS is available at INSDOC, INFLIBNET and DRTC. For further information on training programmes one can contact NISSAT. The training of library staff also depends on the level of automation. If one decides to go only for cataloguing a minimum training of one or two weeks duration will enable the librarians to develop a database and maintain it. With this basic training one can easily transfer the same data on a server/main machine in a network environment. The job becomes easy as most of the institutions have systems department with computer professionals maintaining the network.

Fourthly lack of support from the management, may be owing to budget constraints, will be one of the barriers. Here the role of librarians becomes crucial in convincing the management that the users of libraries will also be the major beneficiaries of automation. Also, the skill and initiative play a major role in convincing the management.

The fifth reason could be retrospective conversion of data. As mentioned earlier the manpower saved could be utilized for retrospective conversion and later on for analytical cataloguing. However, most of the libraries have taken time bound project for this purpose.

Selection of Library Software

As mentioned earlier, if a library wants to make a beginning; CDS/ISIS is best suited as it involves minimum investment on both hardware and software. Once a database with bibliographic details is developed, the same data can be used for circulation activities. Here the selection of software becomes crucial because CDS/ISIS can efficiently handle only the cataloguing system. Following criteria might help the librarians to select the right software for other housekeeping operations:

- Who are the developers, whether an institution, or reputed company or few individuals. The preference is for institution and second preference is for the reputed company. One has to be skeptical about the software developed by individuals as there will be no continuity
- How many times the software has been revised since the time of its first launch.
- How many parameters are available for each module.

More the parameters better will be the flexibility and needs no or minimum customization.

- Whether the software has facility to import bibliographic data available in ISO2709 format and similarly export of data in this format
- Training and guidance after installation
- Whether available on major operating systems.
- Whether it is web ineffaceable
- Whether it can be interfaced with the e-mail system of the campus network.
- Whether it has taken care of Y2K compliant
- How many installations it has got in the country, since when and major clients.
- Whether it can offer OPAC and different rights to different logins.

2

Electronic/Digital Library

What is an electronic journal (or e-journal)- Any journal available over the Internet can be called an "electronic journal" or "e-journal." In many cases e-journals are counterparts to familiar print publications, although an increasing number of titles exist only in electronic format. Frequently e-journals appear on the screen exactly as they do in print with similar page design and typeface. These are PDF (Portable Document Format) images of the print pages. Many users prefer to print from PDF images. To view these page images, your computer must have Adobe Acrobat Reader software installed. You may download the software at no cost by clicking here and following the instructions on the site.

What is the difference between a full-text e-journal and full-text article databases- Full-text e-journals may be viewed as individual issues that correspond to their print counterparts. Typically, you will use these on the publishers' site where you may browse the table of contents of an issue, scan the abstracts of articles, and view the full-text of articles. Full-text article databases are collections of articles, not complete issues of journals. Often these collections bring together articles on a particular subject, such as business or ethnic studies; subject usually searches them.

An electronic library is a heterogeneous system in which information is available in hard copy, on magnetic tape and discs, CD-ROMs and videodiscs, and also from online sources. Storage and copying of information are done either by downloading or by printing from a master file. Such libraries are can provide very diverse information; however, electronic libraries will evolve in an incremental fashion and, at least for the next few decades, we will operate in a dual paper-based and electronic environment.

Digital library collections contain fixed permanent documents. While current libraries have more dynamic collections, a digital library facilitates quicker handling of information. Digital libraries break the physical boundaries of data. Digital libraries are as important for communications and collaboration as for information seeking activities.

Preservation—Libraries have preservation issues of all kinds to deal with, especially the deterioration of the paper collection. Digitizing as a means of preservation is quite beneficial. It helps to preserve rare and fragile objects without denying access to those who wish to study them. Convenience is also a benefit. Users can retrieve digitized books in seconds by searching for words, phrases or ideas. Several people can simultaneously read the same book or view the same picture. Another benefit is space. Electronic copies occupy millimeters of space rather than meters on shelf.Preservation concerns include deciding what to digitize, formats for texts and images, quality of images, and costs.

Technologies—Digitization requires certain technologies. These include storage technologies-a variety of devices to store and retrieve information in digital form such as magnetic tapes/ cassettes, floppy disks, hard disks, DAT Tape, CD-ROM, smart cards; processing technology - creating the systems and applications software that is required for the performance of digital network; communication technologies - primarily to communicate information in digital form; display technologies-varieties of output devices.

E-Journals in India—Most of the world's leading publishers have electronic journal (e-journal) access services at present. IIT Bombay subscribes to the full text versions of 222 e-journals covering a large number of publishers such as Elsevier, AIP, ACS, ASCE, SIAM, ASME,IOP, RSC, OUP, Wiley, etc. These are made available on their intranet. A list of 158 free electronic journals and magazines are also accessible through their site. IIT Madras provides full text access to their clientele to the Science Direct service of Elsevier and the ACM journals, in addition to more than a dozen titles online. IIT Delhi Library has a much wider coverage of full text e-journals. These include Science Direct from Elsevier, IEEE/IEE Electronic library, American Physical Society, AIP, ASCE, Chemweb, etc. Their subscription to a group of eleven bibliographic databases called "Materials Science Collection" from Cambridge Science Abstracts (CSA) is another noteworthy service.

TIFR has the full text facility of all the Springer journals through the LINK service. Some of the CSIR Labs with their individual efforts have already established excellent facilities in e-library operations. Science Direct is already operational in four CSIR Labs i.e., National Chemical Laboratory Pune, National Institute of Oceanography Goa, Central Drug Research Laboratory Trivandrum.

INSDOC, the apex institution for Information System and Services under CSIR runs a Digital Library. The electronic library of INSDOC has a rich collection of about 3,500 foreign science and technology periodicals, including 1,123 full text journals. The Virtual Library operational at the Administrative Staff College of India (ASCI), Hyderabad is perhaps a role model. The Indian Institutes of Management, in Bangalore, Calcutta, Ahmedabad, and elsewhere, are currently in the process of evolving e-journal consortia for their group of libraries.

National Center for Science Information (NCSI) Bangalore plays a unique role in providing access, delivering service, and imparting education in electronic journals and bibliographic databases and a host of other related services/activities. The web-enabled databases/journals include Biosis, Medline, Compendex, Inspec, Mathsci, Current Contents, Adonis (Biomedical Journals),

Cambridge Scientific Abstracts, Chemical Abstracts, Union Catalogue of Publications in Bangalore Libraries, etc. NCSI access to UnCover provides free access to the content pages of over 16,000 journals.

J-Gate, the e-journal portal for scholarly, research, and technical journals launched by M/s. Informatics India Ltd., Bangalore is a solution offered to institutions who do not have adequate expertise and resources for e-journals access at an affordable rate and in a customized package.

E-learning in Digital Libraries—Most of our university libraries are now automated and many scholars have e-mail accounts. Communication and data transfer or interchange has become easy with the help of Internet and email attachments. The Inflibnet program for university libraries is expanding in every dimension. The concept of e learning can be incorporated into a digital library system. For instance, in an e-learning environment the contents are truly dynamic. Any piece of information comes with a system that equips a user to test his level of knowledge. Libraries have adapted accordingly to enhance the learning process.

Some of the Links for E-Journals

1. Providing links to the world's electronic journals: http://www.e-journals.org/
2. Links of different ejournal (Subject wise) : http://scholar.lib.vt.edu/ejournals/
3. Recent Library news, views, technology etc. http://www.libraryjournal.com/
4. Electronics journal Archives: http://www.ifla.org/II/etext.htm
5. Ejournal site guide : www.library.ubc.ca/ejour/ L
6. List of Top International Journals - http://dmoz.org/Reference/Journals/
7. List of Indian Journals in General- http://isidev.nic.in/jrnlist.html

3

Consortia in Libraries

It is a well-known fact that the traditional mode of operation of libraries is in deep crisis. Several developments have contributed to this crisis. Firstly, the continuous price increase for scientific information combined with the lack of funding led to massive yearly cancellations of scientific journals. Secondly, the exponential growth in the production of knowledge has made it more and more impossible for the individual library to purchase all the relevant information. Thirdly, the rapid technological developments have resulted in a constant pressure for new hardware, software and education and training of library staff. Finally, the overwhelming application of new technologies—especially the World Wide Web—in all media has contributed to rapid escalating user expectations in the sense that the users expect library information to be delivered just as fast as any other information they need in their daily lives.

A proper strategy can take advantage of the new developments and contribute to solve the ongoing serials crisis, if the libraries manage to change themselves by adopting consortia. Consortia are regarded as an effective strategy to increase the buying power of individual libraries over the short term and as an opportunity to maximize opportunities for cooperative collection building and for resource sharing over the long term. They offer libraries the ability to give users the access they are coming to expect and demand to a much broader range of materials than any one library could possibly offer. It is now being overheard everywhere. It is more because of electronic or digital form of information. In the

West, Consortia is a thing of the past, where there were models for print journal subscriptions, co-operative resource sharing, etc. But in this electronic age it has gained momentum even in the developing countries.

In the process commercial publishers and scholarly societies are trying to implement the new technologies in their productions processes and services. A number of new journals are only available in electronic format. Publishers, database producers, subscription agents and other intermediaries are already on the market with their own "integrated electronic libraries" - many of these targetted and taylored towards the end user. These products have the potential of bypassing the libraries; some of the producers won't even deal with libraries! Some publishers offer discount to customers who go for electronic products only. This pricing strategy aims at eliminating the print edition in order to save costs in the future. What we are witnessing here is a dramatic change in the production processes and services. These changes require investments on a significant scale both from the producers and the customers. Furthermore at the same time an increased cooperation and competition among publishers, database producers, agents and other intermediaries are taking place. Cooperation in the sense that publishers offer bibliographic data to database producers in order to increase the demand for their electronic full text journals. And competition often leading to mergers or as one can put it: cannibalism where large redundancy operations are taking place.

Now a number of publishers offer consortia—if their purchase power is big enough—access to the whole range of their journals. That is, every member of the consortium will have electronic access not only to the journals currently subscribed to but all the journals. As we all know libraries currently subscribe only to those journals that they can afford on any specific time of date, and there will be a number of other journals of the specific publisher the library occasionally will have to interline as well. Such a consortium agreement will give the library, and therefore also the user, extended access—that is better service—and reduce the costs—that is staff costs and document delivery costs(paper work)—in interblending procedures. In my opinion, the costs for this are usually a modest increase in payments to the publisher.

However there are a number of obstacles for the libraries to take advantage of this development. Firstly, there is the ever-present funding problem. Entering consortia requires initial investments in licenses and information and communication technology. Secondly libraries are not prepared to cash in the savings offered by not handling the print edition of the journals. Their work procedures are still centered around the physical document, staff are not trained in handling electronic documents etc. Therefore many libraries are reluctant in entering consortia agreements especially where publishers impose payments for off-consortia delivery of documents, either in electronic or paper format. Thirdly there will often be investments to be made in local - consortium based - central hardware set up, mounting of data, development of interfaces, administration of access etc. However those problems are precisely to be solved not by the single library but in cooperation between the participating libraries.

Consortia in India

(A) CSIR Consortia: It is a consortium for CSIR Laboratories for accessing e-journals.

- TKDL (Traditional Knowledge Digital Library)
- E-journals Consortia by NISCAIR
- Directory of S&T Awards in India - Updation
- Database of Intramural R&D Projects - Updation

Traditional Knowledge Digital Library (TKDL): India is endowed with immense traditional knowledge, which is either undocumented or available in ancient classical and other literature, often inaccessible to the Information Managers and Patent Examiners. Documentation of this existing knowledge, available in the public domain, on various traditional systems of medicine has become imperative to safeguard its sovereignty and protect it from being misused in patenting of non-original inventions. To address this problem of grave national concern, NISCAIR and the Department of Indian Systems of Medicine and Homoeopathy (ISM&H) have entered into an agreement for establishing a Traditional Knowledge Digital Library (TKDL) on Ayurveda. NISCAIR is the implementing agency for this project. Its responsibilities include providing user-friendly software, setting up TKDL hardware and software platform for data entry, digitizing images of Slokas, making Directory on Traditional Knowledge Resource Classification (TKRC), populating the database and hosting the database in web/portal. TKDL will be available in English, German, French, Spanish and Japanese since these languages account for more than 98% of the international patent applications. This will give legitimacy to the existing traditional knowledge and enable protection of such information from getting patented by the fly-by-night inventors acquiring patents on our traditional knowledge systems. The project is progressing very well. TKDL in the first phase targets Ayurveda. But as a whole it would encompass, in addition to Ayurveda, Siddha, Unani, Yoga, Naturopathy and Folklore medicine.

E-journals Consortia: NISCAIR is the nodal organization for developing a "Consortium for CSIR Laboratories for Accessing e-journals". The activity shall range from creation to monitoring of the access facility of scientific periodicals published by leading international institutions. To start with, an agreement has been signed with, e-journal publisher, M/s Elsevier Science for a period of four years for 1200 journals. Under this scheme, CSIR scientists shall be able to access these journals and download material for their use. Such access to world wide journal resources will play a very vital role and strengthen research and development in CSIR laboratories, thus leading to knowledge generation useful for socio-economic development of the country. The objectives are:

- ➢ to strengthen the pooling, sharing and electronically accessing the CSIR library resources.
- ➢ to provide access to world S&T literature to CSIR labs.
- ➢ to nucleate the culture of electronic access resulting into evolution of digital libraries.

(B) Informatics India Pvt. Ltd. with initiation from three different educational institutes has successfully developed three consortium models. These are-*SNDT University* **conortia** of Library and Information Science Abstracts (LISA) with other six universities, Forum for Resource Sharing in Astronomy and Astrophysics [FORSA] consortia of Kluwer E-journal consortia program with five institutes and ,IIMs consortia of 33 Kluwer journals in management sciences. *Forum for Resource Sharing in Astronomy and Astrophysics [FORSA]* - Electronic access to journals published by few publishers with member and branch libraries has been made possible under this forum.Indian Digital Library of Engineering Science and Technology [INDEST] Consortium: *The Ministry of Human Resource Development (MHRD)* as per the

recommendations of expert group headed by Prof Balakrishnan of IISc has set-up "Consortia-based Subscription to Electronic Resources for Technical Education System in India". This consortia is available in three models. Presently all the IIT's, IISc, NITIE, most of the Regional Engineering colleges and Indian Institute of Management's are its members. The consortium being an open-ended proposition, welcomes institutions to join it on their own for sharing maximum benefits it offers in terms of lower subscription rates and better terms of agreement with the publishers. All electronic resources being subscribed shall be available from the publisher's Website. The membership of the consortium is open to any Private or Government-funded Engineering/Technological/Educational institutions/ Universities for one or more electronic resources. The consortium will charge nominal annual fee for its services.

(C) Inflibnet: Consortium of e-journals among university libraries - Inflibnet under UGC Infonet is planning to have consortium of e-journals subscriptions among the university libraries. It is being planned to provide this service through higher bandwidth of internet connection, which will be given to University libraries in a phased manner.

International

(A) BC Electronic Library Network—The British Columbia Electronic Library Network (ELN) is a partnership between the Province of British Columbia and its post-secondary libraries. ELN's purpose is to develop, promote and maintain system-wide mechanisms that allow post-secondary libraries to meet the expanding information needs of the province's learners and educators, at the lowest possible cost.

(B) Center for Research Libraries [CRL]—It is an international not-for-profit consortium of colleges, universities and libraries that makes available scholarly research resources to users everywhere. CRL is governed by the major research libraries of North America and is funded by fees, grants and contributions.

(C) Illinois Digital Academic Library [IDAL]—Provides high quality collection of full text and image digitized resources that supports instruction, study, and research by students, faculty and staff in all eligible Illinois higher education institutions.

(D) International Coalition of Library Consortia [ICOLC]— It is

an informal, self-organized group comprising (as of September 2000) nearly 150 library consortia from around the world. The Coalition serves primarily higher education institutions by facilitating discussion among consortia on issues of common interest. It conducts regular meetings to keep members informed about new electronic information resources, pricing practices of electronic providers and vendors, and other issues of importance to directors and governing boards of consortia.

(E) South Asia Library Consortia—Members of the Committee on Insitutional Cooperation [CIC] with major South Asia collections joined together in 1993 for a program of cooperative activity that will improve collections on South Asia in the Midwest and access to them. This ensured the development of Digital South Asia library. The library includes good number of Indian and other South Asian countries publications.

4

Library Networking

The explosion in the amount of literature that is available, increases among the number of users and their different needs, and the application of electronic media are forcing libraries to construct and participate in networks. Magnetic tapes, floppy disks, and CD-ROMs provide enough data storage capacity. Retrieval through telecommunications networks and access to international databases are available for searching for information on various subjects. With the advent of networks, remote transmission of texts and graphics, video clips and animated clips are also possible.

Definitions: A library network is broadly described, as a group of libraries coming together with some agreement of understanding to help each other with a view to satisfying the information needs of their clientele. UNISIST II working document defines Information Network as a set of inter-related information systems associated with communication facilities, which are cooperating through more or less formal agreements in order to implement information handling operations to offer better services to the users.

Objectives

- To promote and support adoption of standards in library operations.
- To create databases for projects, specialists and institutions to provide online information services
- To improve the efficiency of housekeeping operations
- To coordinate with other regional, national & international network for exchange of information and documents
- To generate new services and to improve the efficiency of existing ones

Network Development in India: Some factors those are responsible for the development of library and information networks in India are:

- The report of the working group of the planning commission on modernization of library services and informatics for the seventh five year plan, 1985-90
- The National Policy on Library & Information systems document (1986) accepted by the ministry of HRD, Government of India.
- The report on national policy on university libraries prepared by the Association of Indian Universities (1987)
- The UGC report on information systems for science and technology under the Department of Science & Industrial Research (DSIR) Government of India has been vigorously promoting an integrated approach to library automation and networking

Limitations in Network Development- A network may fail in the early stages if there is not proper planning or if adequate funds are not available. Moreover, a common memorandum of agreement signed by the participating libraries at the institutional level is essential for the success of a network venture. On a more practical level, catalog data must be in a standard, machine readable form for it to be shared and exchanged. And, finally, a continuous flow of external assistance is crucial for the network's survival.

Types of Networks: Presently, there are three types of computer networks: LAN, MAN & WAN.

Local Area Network (LAN): A LAN is a number of related computers and electronic devices that share information over a transmission media. A typical use of LAN is to tie together personal computers in an office so that they can all use a single printer and a file server. The LAN can be within a building or a campus wide network.

Metropolitan Area Network (MAN): Attempts are being made to develop this type of network in metropolitan areas such Delhi, Calcutta, Bangalore, Madras, etc.

Wide Area Network (WAN): A large-scale network, involving offices in different cities and countries is referred to as WAN, which is specially designed to interconnect data transmission devices over wide geographical areas.

Categories of Network-Library networks have been divided into two categories: general network and specialized network. The latter can further be divided into metropolitan network and countrywide network.

General Networks In India

NICNET

- Title: National Information Center Network
- Sponsor: Planning Commission, Govt. of India.
- Membership: Four national and regional nodes, 32 state and union territory nodes; seventy cities and towns
- Services: Bulk file transfer; teleconferencing; full text and bibliographic retrieval services
- Application: ICMRNIC Center; MEDLARS in India; Chemical Abstracts database

INDONET

- Title: INDONET data Network
- Sponsor: CMC Ltd (1986) = Informatics India Ltd (1989)
- Membership: Commercial computer network
- Services: Database services such as DIALOG, COMPUSERVE; IP; SHARP
- Applications: ACME; file transfer; international gateway

I - NET (VIKRAM)

- Title: I - NET
- Sponsor: Dept. of Telecommunications, Govt. of India
- Connectivity: Packet switched public data network covering nine cities
- Services: Information exchange through e-mail / FTP; Bibliographic databases
- Specialized Networks
- Metropolitan Networks

CALIBNET

- Title: Calcutta Libraries Network
- Sponsor: NISSAT - Govt. of India
- Applications: Cataloging; serials control; acquisitions; circulation
- Services: CAS; SDI; union catalog; partial database; editing and retrieval of records; global information; search; full-text document delivery; library automation; CALIBNET INFO Services

BONET

- Title: Bombay Library Network
- Sponsor: NISSAT & NCST (1994)
- Objective: To promote cooperation among libraries in Bombay
- Services: online catalog; online document delivery; IRS; interlibrary loan; dissemination of information

DELNET

- Title: Developing Library Network
- Sponsor: NISSAT & NIC (1988)
- Objective: To promote resource sharing; develop a network of libraries; collect, store, disseminate information
- Members: 165 Institutions, 600 Libraries, 15 States in India, 5 from outside India
- Services: resource sharing; free Software; ICE online facility; books database; thesis database; Indian specialists; database

ADINET

- Title: Ahmedabad Library Network
- Sponsor: NISSAT, DSIR (1994) & INFLIBNET
- Objective: To bring cooperation among its regional libraries; to develop databases; to integrate scientific and technical information systems

- Members: nine libraries
- Services: library automation; library holdings; database in progress

MYLIBNET

- Title: Mysore Library Network
- Sponsor: NISSAT (1994)
- Objective: Developing software tools; conducting seminar; workshops/training programs; conduct surveys
- Host Site: CFTRI, Mysore
- Members: 116 Institutions
- Services: MYLIB Database; E-journals; food patents; CFTRI Library Bulletin; public services.
- Countrywide Area Network:

DESINET

- Title: Defence Science Information Network
- Sponsor: DESIDOC, Delhi
- Activity: Focus on scientific, research and defense communities

ERNET

- Title: Educational and Research Network
- Sponsor: Dept. of Electronics, Govt. of India; UNESCO (Financial assistance from UNDP)
- Members: eight institutions (5 IITs, IISc., National Centre for Software Technology - Bombay, CCI wing of Dept. of Electronics)
- Services: Communication services such as e-mail, file transfer, remote log on, database access, bulletin board etc.,

SIRNET

- Title: Scientific and Industrial Research Network
- Sponsor: CSIR (Commissioned Agency- NCST, Bombay)
- Members: 40 labs and R&D Institutions
- Applications: scientific communication; leather technology; natural products; food technology; medicinal Plants

VIDYANET

- Title: VIDYANET (Dedicated Communication Computer Net)
- Sponsor: TATA Institute of Fundamental Research, Bombay

- Objectives: To provide rapid means of communications by linking computers at various institutions in India to similar networks outside the country; to stimulate corporate research, the day-to-day exchange of research information and the execution of joint projects and publications
- Services: File transfer facility; sharing of computer resources and access to remote applications, databases, libraries, etc.

BTISNET

- Title: BTISNET (Specialized Information Network)
- Sponsor: Dept. of Biotechnology, Govt. of India.
- Connectivity: 10 Specialized Information Centres in genetic engineering, plant tissue culture; photosynthesis and plant molecular biology; cell transformation ; bio-process engineering.
- Services: Data processing using applications software; online communication access; facsimile facility

INFLIBNET

- Title: Information Library Network
- Sponsor: UGC (1991)
- Connectivity: computer communication network of universities and R&D; libraries and bibliographic information centers throughout the country
- Members: 200 Universities; 400 College libraries; 200 R&D libraries
- Services: catalog service; database Services; document supply services; e-mail; BBS: audio and video conferencing, etc.

BALNET

- Title: Bangalore Library Network
- Sponsor: JRD;. Tata Memorial Library (1995)
- Members: 100 Libraries

MALIBNET

- Title: Madras Library Network
- Sponsor: INSDOC & NISSAT (1993)
- Members: 15 Libraries
- Activity: Two important databases, a directory database of current serials in Madras and a contents database covering articles published in 300 journals available in Madras libraries.

—

Library Networks Abroad

International programmes like UNISIST of UNESCO, Universal Availability of Publications (UAP) and Universal Access to Information (UAI) of IFLA and a few others have helped in promotion and co-ordination of information services through out the world . Global Information Systems, characterized by decentralized input, centralized processing and decentralized distribution such as INIS, AGRIS & DEVSIS have been evolved towards universal bibliographic control and dissemination of literature. International information networks/centers such as Lockheed/DIALOG, SDI/Orbit & ESA/IRS hold various databases in several disciplines and offer on-line services to users through out the world.

Library Networks in USA

1. On-line Computer Library Center, Dublin, Ohio (OCLC)—Established in 1967, it was formerly known as a Ohio College Library Center. It includes all type of libraries-academic, government, public and special. It has nearly 27,000 libraries as its members.
2. Research Libraries and Information Network (RLIN), Stanford, California—Established in 1978 it supports the co-operative programmes of research libraries group comprising libraries and other research institutions.
3. Western library Network (WLN), Olympia, Washington —Established in 1972 it provides on-line computerized services to promote resource sharing and automated library functions.
4. Besides these, there are various other library networks-SOLINET-Southeastern Library Network , OLC- Oakland library Consortium, Pittsburg, Pennsylvania. Etc.

Networks in UK

1. BLCMP (Birmingham Libraries Co-operative Mechanization Project), Birmingham -It contains 13 million bibliographic records of books, serials, music, maps, Audio-visuals, etc. in its database. There are more than 60 libraries comprising public libraries, college libraries, university libraries and special libraries using its catalogue.

2. LASER (London and South Eastern Library Region)—It is an independent company under the University of London. It promotes library cooperation among 80 libraries in London and South East England and has more than three million records in its database.
3. The British Library —Though not a network, it has nearly 21 databases including BNB(British National Bibliography) holding 15 million bibliographic records. Blaiseline (British Library Automated Information Service)-The automated information service of the British Library services offers search services to its users.

Networks in Canada

1. The National Library of Canada promotes decentralized networking through the use of protocols conforming to the Open System Interconnection (OSI) reference model.—It has nearly 10 million bibliographic records in its online database.
2. CISTI–Canadian Institute for Scientific and Technical Information—It holds books and conference proceedings, over 50,000 serials and millions of technical reports from around the world. Maintains union catalogue of 50,000 serial titles with over 20,000 current titles.
3. UTLAS International Canada- formerly University of Toronto Library Automation System —Established in 1971, it was the first library network utility in North America to go private by becoming a subsidiary of International Thomson Library Services (ITLS)

Australian Libraries Gateway

The Australian Libraries Gateway (ALG) is a free Web-based directory service which has improved access to information about more than 5,400 Australian libraries, their collections and services since March 1998. It aims to be a directory of current information about every library in Australia , a tool for world-wide users, for both library professionals and the general public.

5

World Wide Web/Internet

World Wide Web or Internet, computer-based (computer-mediated) worldwide information network. The Internet is composed of a large number of smaller interconnected networks called internets. These internets may connect tens, hundreds, or thousands of computers, enabling them to share information with each other and to share various resources, such as powerful supercomputers and databases of information. The Internet has made it possible for people all over the world to effectively and inexpensively communicate with each other. Unlike traditional broadcasting media, such as radio and television, the Internet is a decentralized system. Each connected individual can communicate with anyone else on the Internet, can publish ideas, and can sell products with a minimum overhead cost. In the future, the Internet may have a dramatic impact on higher education and business as more universities offer courses and more companies offer goods and services online.The internets from which the Internet is composed are usually public access networks, meaning that the resources of the network can be shared with anyone logging on to, or accessing, the network.

Other types of Internet, called intranets, are closed to public use. Intranets are the most common type of computer network used in companies and organizations where it is important to restrict access to the information contained on the network or (Local Area Network) LAN. During the 1990s the Internet has grown tremendously in the number of people using it and the amount of information contained on it. According to the Internet Society, a non-profit society that studies and promotes the use of the Internet, 134 countries had full Internet connection and an additional 52 countries had limited access (for example, e-mail only) in 1996.

From the late 1960s to the early 1990s, the Internet was a communication and research tool used almost exclusively for academic and military purposes. This changed radically with the introduction of the World Wide Web (also called the WWW, or W3) in 1989. The WWW is a set of programs, standards, and protocols governing the way in which multimedia files (documents that may contain text, photographs, graphics, video, and audio) are created and displayed on the Internet. The Internet contains the WWW and also includes all the hardware (computers, supercomputers, and connections) and non-WWW software and protocols on which the WWW runs. The difference between the Internet and the WWW is similar to the distinction between a computer and a multimedia program that runs on the computer. The explosion in use and popularity of the Internet in the 1990s is most likely due to the graphics-intensive nature of the World Wide Web.

How The Internet Works

The Internet is based on the concept of a client-server relationship between computers, also called a client/server architecture. In a client/server architecture, some computers act as servers, or information providers, while other computers act as clients, or information receivers. The client/server architecture is not one-to-one—that is, a single client computer may access many different servers, and a single server may be accessed by a number of different client computers. To access information on the Internet, a user must first log on, or connect, to the client computer's host network. A host network is a network that the client computer is part of, and is usually a local area network (LAN). Once a connection has been established, the user may request information from a remote server. If the information requested by the user resides on one of the computers on the host network, that information is quickly retrieved and sent to the user's terminal. If the information requested by the user is on a server that does not belong to the host LAN, then the host network connects to other networks until it makes a connection with the network containing the requested server.

In the process of connecting to other networks, the host may need to access a router, a device that determines the best connection path between networks and helps networks to make connections. Once the client computer makes a connection with the server containing the requested information, the server sends the information to the client in the form of a file. A special computer program called a browser enables the user to view the file. Examples of Internet browsers are Mosaic, Netscape, and Internet Explorer. Most Internet files are multimedia documents—that is, text, graphics, photographs, audio, and video may be combined in a single document.

The process of retrieving files from a remote server to the user's terminal is called downloading. One of the strengths of the Internet is that it is structured around the concept of hypertext. The term hypertext is used to describe an interlinked system of documents in which a user may jump from one document to another in a nonlinear, associative way. The ability to jump from one document to the next is made possible through the use of hyperlinks—portions of the hypertext document that are linked to other related documents on the Internet. By clicking on the hyperlink, the user is immediately connected to the document specified by the link. Multimedia files on the Internet are called hypermedia documents.

Accessing the Internet

Access to the Internet falls into two broad categories: dedicated access and dial-up access. With dedicated access, the computer is directly connected to the Internet via a router, or the computer is part of a network linked to the Internet. With dial-up access, a computer connects to the Internet with a temporary connection, generally over a telephone line using a modem—a device that converts the electrical signals from a computer into signals that can be transmitted over traditional telephone lines. A modem is needed because computers are digital, meaning that their signals are made up of discrete units, while most telephone lines are analog, meaning that they carry signals that are continuous instead of discrete. Once a signal has traveled over the telephone line, a second modem is required at the other end of the line to reconvert the transmitted signals from analog to digital. A great many companies, called Internet Service Providers (ISPs), provide dial-up access to the Internet for a modest fee. Examples of ISPs are America Online (AOL), the Microsoft Network (MSN), and CompuServe.

Packaging Information

All data transmitted over the Internet is divided up into small units of information called packets, each of which is labeled with a unique number indicating its place in the data stream—the flow of information between computing devices. When the various packets that make up a set of data arrive at their destination, they are re-assembled using the unique labels given them. Other features make sure that all the data packets arrive intact, automatically requesting that missing or incomplete packets be re-sent from the source. This system, called packet switching, uses a series of protocols, or rules, known as TCP/IP (Transmission Control Protocol/Internet Protocol).

Network Addressing

To be part of the Internet a computer must have a unique Internet Protocol (IP) network address so that messages can be correctly routed to and from the machine over the Internet. Internet addresses are called URLs (Uniform Resource Locators) or DNS (Domain Name System).

History: The Internet is an extension of a computer network originally formed in the United States during the 1960s by the Advanced Research Projects Agency (ARPA). Working under contract to the U.S. Department of Defense, ARPA initially connected computers at the Stanford Research Institute in California, the University of California at Los Angeles (UCLA), the University of California at Santa Barbara (UCSB), and the University of Utah. This original network, the very first computer network, was called ARPANET (ARPA NETwork). As ARPANET grew in the 1970s, with more and more universities and institutions connecting to it, users found it necessary to establish standards for the way that data was transmitted over the network. To meet the needs of data transmission standards, computer scientists developed the Transmission Control Protocol (TCP) and the Internet Protocol (IP). During the 1970s various government, scientific, and academic groups developed their own networks. Examples include the Department of Energy's (DoE) Magnetic

Fusion Energy Network (MFENet), the High Energy Physics NETwork (HEPNET), and the National Science Foundation NETwork (see NSFNET). In 1989 English computer scientist Timothy Berners-Lee introduced the World Wide Web. Berners-Lee initially designed the WWW to aid communication between physicists who were working in different parts of the world for the European Laboratory for Particle Physics (CERN). As it grew, however, the WWW revolutionized the use of the Internet. During the early 1990s increasingly large numbers of users who were not part of the scientific or academic communities began to use the Internet, due in large part to the ability of the WWW to easily handle multimedia documents.

The Future of the Internet: A major challenge facing the continued growth of the Internet is the difficulty of providing enough bandwidth to sustain the network. As Internet applications become more sophisticated, and as more people around the world use the Internet, the amount of information transmitted across the Internet will demand very high bandwidth connections. While many communications companies are attempting to develop higher bandwidth technologies, it is not known whether the technology will be able to satisfactorily keep up with demand.

In order to accommodate the increasing number of users, the non-profit organization University Corporation for Advanced Internet Development (UCAID) is working on the construction of Internet 2. Internet 2 will add more bandwidth, or available communication lines, to the current information superhighway in order to accommodate larger packets of data. UCAID members include representatives from universities, the government, and the computer industry.

Another important question facing Internet growth is the issue of censorship. Because the Internet has grown so rapidly, governments have been slow to regulate its use and to pass laws regarding what content is acceptable. Many Internet users also see such laws as an infringement on their right to free speech. In 1996 the Congress of the United States passed the Communications Decency Act, which made it a crime to transmit indecent material over the Internet. This decision resulted in an immediate outcry from users, industry experts, and civil liberties groups opposed to such censorship. In 1997 the United States Supreme Court declared the act to be unconstitutional because it violated 1st Amendment rights to free speech.

Commercial use of the Internet is sure to grow dramatically as more individuals gain access to it. It may be possible in the future to order nearly any goods from Internet sites and have them delivered using the postal service. Many companies are worried about security issues and the possibility of losing money through Internet commerce. They are therefore being very cautious about doing business on the Internet. Other businesses, however, are embracing the Internet, hoping to be first in what may be a rapidly expanding market.

The issue of business being conducted over the Internet raises important security issues. Companies doing business over the Internet must have very sophisticated security measures in place so that information such as credit card, bank account, and social security numbers cannot be accessed by unauthorized users. (see Computer Security) Similarly, government facilities, universities, and institutions must ensure that access to their computers over the Internet is strictly regulated.

6

Library VS. Internet

We live in the information age, where access to many wonderful Internet resources is just a few quick clicks away. In this age libraries and information centers are slowly becoming storehouse of digital information or electronics based information. Modern libraries prefer computer bases activities and now dependent upon internet/intranet to browse - web OPAC, e - books/journal, databases, needed information through websites, access to libraries of other etc. For this reason, one might be thinking, "Cool. I don't have to go to the library. I can do all my research online." Not so fast. The Internet is not a substitute for the library. It's a tool best used in addition to traditional research sources. Why use both? Because each has resources, benefits, and limitations that the other does not. Examine the pros and cons of both the library and the Internet below.

Pros (Library)

1. Uses universal cataloging systems that classify and organize all resources.
2. Houses professional books, newspapers, magazines, and other resources that have been edited and reviewed prior to their publication.
3. Provides free access to journals, magazines, newspapers, encyclopedias, and other print reference works.
4. Often has archived materials—newspapers and magazines—that date back many years.
5. Offers a free Internet connection and other electronic resources, such as reference CD-ROMs.
6. Has knowledgeable reference librarians to help you locate resources.

Pros (Internet)

1. Online resources can be accessed 24 hours a day, 7 days a week.
2. Web sites can be constantly updated to provide breaking news and timely information.
3. Provides opportunities for two-way communication through e-mail, LISTSERVS, and newsgroups.
4. Provides access to many newspapers, magazines, journals, and encyclopedias.
5. Some sites feature rare books, documents, and special collections that traditionally have only been available in libraries.
6. Offers a complete multimedia experience, with text, video, interactive features, audio, hyperlinks, and graphics all in one place.

Cons (Library & Internet)

In a library resources can be checked out by other patrons and, therefore, may not always be available. A library's publications cannot provide up-to-the-minute news and information the way Web sites can. Closes after hours. On the other hand Internet has no system that catalogs and organizes all resources. Anyone with an Internet connection can publish a Web site. It is reliability of information is not guaranteed. Archived materials might only date back several years. Some electronic resources are only available through a subscription. Internet access is often not free. Does not have knowledgeable librarians who can help you find resources and excessive use of internet may clogs up networks and slows down the transmission of information. On the other hand the Internet resources contain different types of materials, but a chunk of it is highly controversial in nature. It is very difficult task to censor access to offensive information. Hence cyber crimes are coming into existence.

7

Reasons Why the Internet is No Substitute for a Library

Reading, said the great English essayist Matthew Arnold, "is culture." Given the condition of reading test scores among school children nationwide, it isn't surprising to find both our nation and our culture in trouble. Further, the rush to Internetize all schools, particularly K–12, adds to our downward spiral. If it were not for the Harry Potter books one might lose all hope who languishes here. Then, suddenly, you realize libraries really are in trouble, grave danger, when important higher-education officials opine, "Don't you know the Internet has made libraries obsolete?" Gadzooks! as Harry himself might say. In an effort to save our culture, strike a blow for reading, and, above all, correct the well-intentioned but horribly misguided notions about what is fast becoming Intertopia among many nonlibrarian bean counters, here are 10 reasons why the Internet is no substitute for a library.

1. Not Everything Is on the Internet

With over one billion Web pages you couldn't tell it by looking. Nevertheless, very few substantive materials are on the Internet for free. For example, only about 8% of all journals are on the Web, and an even smaller fraction of books are there. Both are costly! If you want the Journal of Biochemistry, Physics Today, Journal of American History, you'll pay, and to the tune of hundreds of thousands of dollars.

2. The Needle (Your Search) in the Haystack (the Web)

The Internet is like a vast uncataloged library. Whether you're using Hotbot, Lycos, Dogpile, Infoseek, or any one of a dozen other search or metasearch engines, you're not searching the entire Web. Sites often promise to search everything but they can't deliver. Moreover, what they do search is not updated daily, weekly, or even monthly, regardless of what's advertised. If a librarian told you, "Here are 10 articles on Native Americans. We have 40 others but we're not going to let you see them, not now, not yet, not until you've tried another search in another library," you'd throw a fit. The Internet does this routinely and no one seems to mind.

3. Quality Control Doesn't Exist

Yes, we need the Internet, but in addition to all the scientific, medical, and historical information (when accurate), there is also a cesspool of waste. When young people aren't getting their sex education off XXX-rated sites, they're learning politics from the Freeman Web page, or race relations from Klan sites. There is no quality control on the Web, and there isn't likely to be any. Unlike libraries where vanity press publications are rarely, if ever, collected, vanity is often what drives the Internet. Any fool can put up anything on the Web, and, to my accounting, all have.

4. What You Don't Know Really Does Hurt You

The great boon to libraries has been the digitization of journals.

But full-text sites, while grand, aren't always full. What you don't know can hurt you: articles on these sites are often missing, among other things, footnotes; tables, graphs, and formulae do not often show up in a readable fashion (especially when printed); and journal titles in a digitized package change regularly, often without warning. A library may begin with X number of journals in September and end with Y number in May. Trouble is, those titles aren't the same from September to May. Although the library may have paid $100,000 for the access, it's rarely notified of any changes. I would not trade access to digitized journals for anything in the world, but their use must be a judicious, planned, and measured one, not full, total, and exclusive reliance.

5. States Can Now Buy One Book and Distribute to Every Library on the Web—NOT!

Yes, and we could have one national high school, a national university, and a small cadre of faculty teaching everybody over streaming video. Let's take this one step further and have only digitized sports teams for real savings! (Okay, I know, I've insulted the national religion.) Since 1970 about 50,000 academic titles have been published every year. Of these 1.5 million titles, fewer than a couple thousand are available. What is on the Net are about 20,000 titles published before 1925. Why? No copyright restrictions that cause prices to soar to two or three times their printed costs. Finally, vendors delivering e-books allow only one digitized copy per library. If you check out an e-book over the Web, I can't have it until you return it. Go figure, as they say. And if you're late getting the book back, there is no dog-ate-my-homework argument. It's charged to your credit card automatically.

6. Hey, Bud, You Forgot about E-book Readers

Most of us have forgotten what we said about microfilm ("It would shrink libraries to shoebox size"), or when educational television was invented ("We'll need fewer teachers in the future"). Try reading an e-book reader for more than a half-hour. Headaches and eyestrain are the best results. Besides, if what you're reading is more than two pages long, what do you do? Print it. Where's a tree hugger when you really need one? Moreover, the cost of readers runs from $200 to $2,000, the cheaper ones being harder on the eyes. Will this change? Doubtless, but right now there's no market forces making it change. Will it change in less than 75 years? Unlikely!

7. Aren't There Library-less Universities Now?

No. The newest state university in California at Monterey opened without a library building a few years ago. For the last two years, they've been buying books by the tens of thousands because—surprise, surprise—they couldn't find what they needed on the Internet. California Polytechnic State University, home of the world's highest concentration of engineers and computer geeks, explored the possibility of a virtual (fully electronic) library for two years. Their solution was a $42-million traditional library with, of course, a strong electronic component. In other words, a fully virtualized library just can't be done. Not yet, not now, not in our lifetimes.

8. But a Virtual State Library Would Do It, Right?

Do what, bankrupt the state? Yes, it would. The cost of having everything digitized is incredibly high, costing tens of millions of dollars just in copyright releases. And this buys only one virtual library at one university. Questia Media, the biggest such outfit, just spent $125 million digitizing 50,000 books released (but not to libraries!) in January. At this rate, to virtualize a medium-sized library of 400,000 volumes would cost a mere $1,000,000,000! Then you need to make sure students have equitable access everywhere they need it, when they need it. Finally, what do you do with rare and valuable primary sources once they are digitized? Take them to the dump? And you must hope the power never, ever goes out. Sure, students could still read by candlelight, but what would they be reading?

9. The Internet: A Mile Wide, an Inch (or Less) Deep

Looking into the abyss of the Internet is like vertigo over a void. But the void has to do not only with what's there, but also with what isn't. Not much on the Internet is more than 15 years old. Vendors offering magazine access routinely add a new year while dropping an earlier one. Access to older material is very expensive. It'll be useful, in coming years, for students to know (and have access to) more than just the scholarly materials written in the last 10 to15 years.

10. The Internet Is Ubiquitous but Books Are Portable

In a recent survey of those who buy electronic books, more than 80% said they like buying paper books over the Internet, not reading them on the Web. We have nearly 1,000 years of reading print in our bloodstream and that's not likely to change in the next 75. Granted, there will be changes in the delivery of electronic materials now, and those changes, most of them anyway, will be hugely beneficial. But humankind, being what it is, will always want to curl up with a good book—not a laptop—at least for the foreseeable future.

The Web is great; but it's a woefully poor substitute for a full-service library. It is mad idolatry to make it more than a tool. Libraries are icons of our cultural intellect, totems to the totality of knowledge. If we make them obsolete, we've signed the death warrant to our collective national conscience, not to mention sentencing what's left of our culture to the waste bin of history. No one knows better than librarians just how much it costs to run a library. We're always looking for ways to trim expenses while not contracting service. The Internet is marvelous, but to claim, as some now do, that it's making libraries obsolete is as silly as saying shoes have made feet unnecessary.(This article originally appeared in American Libraries, April 2001, p. 76–78.)

8

Internet Search Tips and Strategies

The Internet has an enormous quantity of information, with thousands of newsgroups and billions of web pages. The two questions that face any information seeker are, (1) How can I find what I want? and (2) How can I know that what I find is any good? This article treats the first question. A companion article,

"Evaluating Internet Research Sources," treats the second. Through the use of a little creativity, some patience, and a few search engines, you will be able to find just about anything you want. Many of the search tools and tool types mentioned in this article are available at "World Wide Web Research Tools." Before this let us know about the categories of information on web.

Categories of Information on the Web: Before you begin searching, you first need a little understanding about how information is stored and accessed on the Web. There are basically three categories of information on the Web:

1. *The Free, Visible Web.* This category includes all the publicly mounted Web pages. These pages are indexed by search engines. To find information from this category, use a good search engine or directory.
2. *The Free, Invisible Web.* This category includes the contents of sites that provide their articles or information free to users, but that content may be accessible only by going directly to the site. In other words, search engines cannot index it. Some magazines, newspapers, reference works, and other sites are in this category. Many databases such as legal, medical, and financial are here, too. To find information from this category, you must go to the appropriate database.
3. *Paid Databases over the Web.* This category includes commercial databases that libraries subscribe to, containing scholarly journals, newspapers, court cases and the like. Providers like Lexis-Nexis, UMI Proquest, Infotrac, JSTOR and others are in this group. To find information from this category, you must have access to the database (through password or an on-campus computer) and search on the database directly.

Search Tool Types: Search tools fall into three main categories. (Note that a given search site may combine tools, since sites are in a constant state of change, merging, and partnering.)

- *Search Engines.* A search engine consists of the interface you use to type in a query, an index of Web sites that the query is matched with, and a software program (called a spider or bot) that goes out on the Web and gets new sites for the index. The bot crawls the Web at certain intervals, in order to index new material. When you use a search engine, you are asking it to look in its index to find matches with the words you have typed in. Some search engines index not only the World Wide Web, but also Usenet newsgroups. Many search engines are now becoming reference sites which contain much more than just search capability. They may also have news, weather, free software, picture indexes, ratings of web sites, and other features. There are several hundred search engines, but they fall into a handful of types:

1. *Global.* This type of engine, typified by Google, Fast Search, Northern Light, HotBot, AltaVista, and others, reads pages from all over the world in many languages. These engines may index more than a billion pages.
2. *Regional.* Some search engines are limited geographically. For example, only information on Web sites in Australia may be indexed.
3. *Targeted.* These search engines limit themselves to one subject, like biography, medicine, graphics, art, fishing, and so forth.
4. *Reference.* These provide information from a set of reference works, such as an encyclopedia. Britannica, Bartleby and xrefer are examples.

➢ Directories. Directories are categorized lists of sites picked out by human editors. Directory databases are therefore much smaller than those of search engines. However, the fact that the sites are hand picked often means that you will find very high quality sites or articles in the results. Example directories are Yahoo, Look Smart, and Snap.

Quick Guide to Choosing a Starting Place: Here are some suggestions about where to start a search.

➢ I've got a broad subject in mind, but don't know exactly what I'm interested in or how to look it up. For broad subjects, such as information processing, Tibet, photosynthesis, volcanoes, Samuel Johnson, rope making and so on, try an encyclopedia or similar reference site.

➢ I need information about a general subject area. To find information about business, law, medicine, old master paintings, government documents and so forth, use a targeted search engine.

➢ I have a well-known specific subject in mind and want to find some relevant sites. To find sites for subjects such as Hawaiian vacations, exercise routines, colleges and universities in California, dietary guidelines, art museums, try a directory.

- I need information on a very specific and unusual subject. To find information about tea tree oil, Chihuahua coughing, paradichlorobenzine, or the Airbus 320, use a general search engine.
- I am doing a research paper and need substantial information from many sources. For serious research, use a combination of several search engines, directories, and other tools. Read on for further help.

Word Searches With Search Engines

As mentioned above, search engines index the exact words found on Web pages. Thus, when you search with a search engine, you are looking for exact words. "Choose your words well," says the proverb. Since you do not know exactly what words may be on a particular Web page that covers the subject you are interested in, you must be creative in anticipating the possibilities. There are several ways to type in a word search. Knowing the differences can help you get better results.

1. *Keyword Search*. Many search engines by default offer a keyword search. This kind of search will find all pages that contain any of the words you have specified. Moreover, the search will find the words in any order and in any location. For example, suppose you are looking for information about the formulas in shampoo. If you perform a keyword search using the phrase consumer product chemistry, the engine will return every page that mentions any one of these three words anywhere on the page. Thus, you will see pages about "Consumer Protest over Dangerous Toys," and so forth. Fortunately, most engines list their findings (hits) in a ranked order, so that hits with all of the words will be listed before hits with only one or two of the words. And usually, pages where the words are close together will be listed earlier. However, that still means that your keyword search for consumer product chemistry will return a page containing, "Some consumer groups are advocating product warning labels on children's chemistry sets."

2. *Phrase Search*. Many search engines allow you to perform an exact phrase search, so that pages with only the words you type in, in that exact order and with no words in between them,

will be found. The exact phrase search is often a remedy for too many irrelevant hits. To perform an exact phrase search at a search engine that permits it, put the phrase in quotation marks: "consumer product chemistry." If you get zero results, go back to the Forest Log and do some work!

3. Boolean Operators. Named after mathematician George Boole, Boolean logic involves the operators AND, OR, NOT, and occasionally NEAR. These operators are available in some engines to expand or contract your search results. The operator OR expands the search, while the others contract it. Let me explain by examples. If you type into the search engine, "summer OR flowers," you will get a hit on every page that has either the word "summer" or the word "flowers" on it. (For the technically minded, the OR is an inclusive OR so that pages with both words will also be returned.) On the other hand, if you type in, "summer AND flowers," only pages with both terms will be returned. As you might imagine, this will be a smaller set of hits. If you type in "summer NOT flowers," then only pages with the word "summer" and not with the word "flowers" will be found. And similarly, if you type in "summer NEAR flowers," only pages with the word "summer" in the close vicinity of the word "flowers" will be returned. Some pages allow you to specify the nearness of the words, such as not more than 15 or 50 words apart.

Search Tips

1. *Use several search tools.* Because of the constant indexing that search sites do, and because of the way their indexes work, some will find content that others will not. No engine has the entire Web indexed. Use several engines and several directories, and look at reference and targeted engines as well for the most thorough search. (And remember the Invisible Web!). See "World Wide Web Research Tools" for a list of good engines and other tools.
2. *Read the search tips or help information at each search engine.* You will learn how to perform more sophisticated searches, how to restrict or expand searches, and how to use the site more efficiently. For example, AltaVista, Excite, and InfoSeek allow the use of quotation marks to create an exact phrase search, a plus sign to indicate a word that must occur to yield a hit page, and a minus sign to exclude

pages that include the word. By combining these items, you can create a very powerful and specific search: "lesson plans" +K-12 -science tells the engine to search for the exact phrase lesson plans (rather than just the two words anywhere in the document, on pages that must include the term K-12 and that must not include the word science.

3. *For keyword searches, use several words.* If you type in a general topic word as if you were looking through a card catalog, you are likely to receive tens or even hundreds of thousands of hits. A search for "insomnia," for example, will return more than 20,000 hits from one engine. You might try a search on "causes insomnia cure better sleep sleepless" or something similar. Try to imagine what words might occur in an article you want and type in several of those words. Use synonyms, too. Alternatively, use an exact phrase search on "treatment of insomnia" or a directory search, starting with the subject Health or Lifestyle. Note that you can combine various phrases into one search to improve your yield. If you are researching apple growing, you might combine several phrases from different places on the ladder of generalization and type in fruit tree apple farming growing Washington Red Delicious orchards Gala Fuji Granny Smith and see what you get.

4. *Guess a location.* The address or URL (uniform resource locator) of a web site is, surprisingly, often guessable. Many companies use a standard form of URL, which is http://www.companynamehere.com, where "companynamehere" is the name of the company. Thus, for exampie, Sony is found at http://www.sony.com and you can figure out how to get to Disney, Honda, and NBC the same way. Companies with long names often abbreviate them in some guessable way, as for example http://www.nytimes.com is the New York Times, and the standard form with "adage" in the middle will bring up Advertising Age and with "popsci" in the middle will get you Popular Science. Moreover, that middle word is often the key to a site's content even when not identifying a famous company. What, for example, do you think you would find at http://www.fraud.com or http://www.weather.com? Try the standard form with "salami" or even "search" and see what happens. Try a few of your own areas, based on a topic (like news) an item (like a fruit), or a place.

5. *Select the wheat from the chaff by thinking about what you want. What are you looking for?* Facts, opinions (anyone's opinion or an

expert's), statistics, narratives of personal experience, eyewitness descriptions, new ideas, proven solutions, reference material? See the companion article, "Evaluating Internet Research Sources" for more information.

6. *Back up to find out where you are.* When you click on a hit from a search engine, you are connected directly to the page where the search terms were matched. It is not always clear exactly where you have arrived. You may see something like, "Chapter 5: The Triumph of Palladian Architecture." Who wrote this? What is the book about, of which this is Chapter 5? To answer these questions, look at the URL (address) you have connected to. If may look something like this: http://www.some.edu/faculty/jones/architec/ch5.htm. The page you are reading is the lowest level of a series of directories beginning with the web site (www.some.edu), dropping to a "faculty" directory, then to a "jones" directory, and so on. To learn more about the context of your Chapter 5, go to the right end of the URL and chop off the "ch5.htm" and then press return. This will have the effect of backing you up one level in the hierarchy and you can see what the higher directory ("architec" in this case) is all about. You might find a book title, author, or other information. Now chop off the "architec" directory and back up to "jones" to see what is there. Back up as far as you want or need to in order to find out the information you need about the work and its author. If you are doing research for a report or project, be sure to write down the URL and all pertinent information so that you can cite the source properly.If you print directly from your browser, the URL will be printed for you in an upper or lower corner. But if you save the page to disk, the URL will not be included, so be sure to copy it down.

Lifesaver tip: If you accidentally neglect to write down the URL, but have a printed or disk copy of the article, you can either see the URL printed at the top of the page or you can use a search engine to locate the article for you again. To do this, type in from the article a four or five-word phrase that contains the most unusual words you can find. Then perform an exact phrase search for these words. The engine will almost always take you right to the article.

9

TQM in Libraries

"The function of a harp player is to play the harp. The function of good harp player is to play it well." – Aristotle.

In the 1950s, the Japanese asked W. Edwards Deming, an American statistician and management theorist, to help them improve their war torn economy. By implementing Deming's principles of total quality management (TQM), Japan experienced dramatic economic growth. In the 1980s, when the United States began to see a reduction in its own world market share in relation to Japan, American business rediscovered Deming. Quality management experts, Joseph Juran and Philip Crosby, also contributed to the development of TQM theories, models, and tools. TQM is now practiced in business as well as in government, the military, education, and in non-profit organizations including libraries (Jurow & Barnard, 1993).

TQM is "a system of continuous improvement employing participative management and centered on the needs of customers" (Jurow & Barnard, 1993). Key components of TQM are employee involvement and training, problem solving teams, statistical methods, long-term goals and thinking, and recognition that the system, not people, produces inefficiencies. Libraries can benefit from TQM in three ways: breaking down interdepartmental barriers; redefining the beneficiaries of library services as internal customers (staff) and external customers (patrons); and reaching a state of continuous improvement (Jurow & Barnard, 1993).

STEPS TO TOTAL QUALITY MANAGEMENT: Based on his work with Japanese managers and others, Deming (1986; Walton,

1986) outlined 14 steps that managers in any type of organization can take to implement a total quality management program.

1. Create constancy of purpose for improvement of product and service. Contancy of purpose requires innovation, investment in research and education, continuous improvement of product and service, maintenance of equipment, furniture and fixtures, and new aids to production.
2. Adopt the new philosophy. Management must undergo a transformation and begin to believe in quality products and services.
3. Cease dependence on mass inspection. Inspect products and services only enough to be able to identify ways to improve the process.
4. End the practice of awarding business on price tag alone. The lowest priced goods are not always the highest quality; choose a supplier based on its record of improvement and then make a long-term commitment to it.
5. Improve constantly and forever the system of product and service. Improvement is not a one-time effort; management is responsible for leading the organization into the practice of continual improvement in quality and productivity.
6. Institute training and retraining. Workers need to know how to do their jobs correctly even if they need to learn new skills.
7. Institute leadership. Leadership is the job of management. Managers have the responsibility to discover the barriers that prevent staff from taking pride in what they do. The staff will know what those barriers are.
8. Drive out fear. People often fear reprisal if they "make waves" at work. Managers need to create an environment where workers can express concerns with confidence.
9. Break down barriers between staff areas. Managers should promote teamwork by helping staff in different areas/ departments work together. Fostering interrelationships among departments encourages higher quality decision-making.
10. Eliminate slogans, exhortations, and targets for the workforce. Using slogans alone, without an investigation

into the processes of the workplace, can be offensive to workers because they imply that a better job could be done. Managers need to learn real ways of motivating people in their organizations.

11. Eliminate numerical quotas. Quotas impede quality more than any other working condition; they leave no room for improvement. Workers need the flexibility to give customers the level of service they need.
12. Remove barriers to pride of workmanship. Give workers respect and feedback about how they are doing their jobs.
13. Institute a vigorous program of education and retraining. With continuous improvement, job descriptions will change. As a result, employees need to be educated and retrained so they will be successful at new job responsibilities.
14. Take action to accomplish the transformation. Management must work as a team to carry out the previous 13 steps.

Total quality management is an approach that an organisation takes for improving its performance on systematic and continuous basis. This is achieved by involving all employees throughout the organisation in satisfying all requirements of every customer, whoever the customer may be - either external or internal. Quality management is the basis for library management in general. Such principles of TQM as meeting the customers needs, exact assessment, continuous improvement, teamwork, and enthusiasm of the leaders are typical for library service.

Total—everyone in the organisation is involved in creating and maintaining the quality of the services and products offered.

Quality—the organisation through individual and collective actions focuses on meeting customer needs, recognising that customer perception identifies quality.

Management—in managing the system, the emphasis lies on continuously improving the system in order to achieve the best results.

TQM is a management philosophy embracing all activities through which the needs of the customer and the community, and the objectives of the organisation, are satisfied in the most efficient and cost-effective way by maximizing the potential of all employees in a continuing drive for improvement (Metreveli, 1998).

Why Libraries Should Adapt TQM

Libraries are among the most ancient social and cultural institutions in existence. Ancient libraries as well as modern ones have one thing in common: all of them have a body of information recorded on some type of medium and that information could be retrieved when needed. The accessibility of information requires good organisational ability from those who are in charge. The basic concern is to create a structure of the organisation where desired information is retrieved and made accessible efficiently and in a timely manner to the users. Creation and maintenance of such a structure requires an effective management process that facilitates work toward that goal.

Over many centuries libraries have adopted many different management principles from business, industry, religion, and government. A library is a business that must be operated efficiently and well. A major difference is that most libraries are non-profit organisations. Management of vast amounts of information stored in different formats - printed, electronic, audio, video - requires use of the most modern management techniques.

Today technologies have changed our social and economic life. In the workplace methodologies change; people work at home or on the web with flexible timetables, and more and more virtual communities are emerging in different fields. The most important stakeholders in the library are customers, the providers of subsidies, staff, and other libraries. These stakeholders are interested, for various reasons, in the introduction of TQM. The introduction of TQM makes great demands on the staff. The following factors in particular need to be taken into account:

- TQM involves a process of change and therefore requires of staff that they be ready to play a constructive role in that process.
- TQM requires a basic reorientation from the media stock towards customers and markets. For TQM a result-oriented approach, not the input of resources, is of vital importance.
- A strongly hierarchical organisation with fragmented responsibilities is not well suited to the introduction of TQM since all staff needs to feel a responsibility for influencing quality.

- ➢ The effort necessary for implementing TQM is at the same time rewarding for both staff and the institution: improvement of the institution in which they work, a strengthening of that institution's position, and more opportunity of staff to influence their own work (Klaassen & Wiersma).

The management of quality in libraries, as a management method that allows the improvement of performance, has been the object of interest for the managers of these services. In this context, the identification of indicators that may take into account the social-economical and political context that permeate the reality of the information services is essential to better adequate the quality proposals.

TQM in India

As a response of this challenge of quality, India's University Grants Commission (UGC) has set up NAAC (National Accreditation and Assessment Council). NAAC conducts audits and inspections on the quality of service provided by educational institutions, including library service. Grants are linked to the outcomes of these assessments. In light of this, academic libraries must develop systems, philosophies, and strategies for managing quality. The primary purpose of an academic library is to support the teaching, research, and other academic programs of its parent organization. An academic library is part of a service organization, which delivers products personally to the customer. In a manufacturing concern, the customer is remote, where as in service organization like an academic library, producers and consumer meet face to face. The complexity of managing service organizations is typically compounded by the existence of multiple interfaces.

Managing Quality in Libraries: In a service organization like libraries, customer satisfaction means fulfilling expectations. Librarians must find out what readers want and concentrate upon providing it. Designing an appropriate service means asking:

- ➢ Who are the customers?
- ➢ What do they want?
- ➢ What can the organization provide?

In a library there are basically two types of customer: those who are in hurry and those who want to kill time. An academic library has to identify these and serve them accordingly.

Managing Customer Expectations: The expectations that the customers bring to a library have a critical effect upon their perceptions of quality. It is better to acquire a reputation for one or two factors which are important to customers and to concentrate upon developing those.

1. Service delivery is like a theoretical performance. If customers are to gain maximum benefit from a service, they must know how to use it. So, properly planned user education is a must for an academic library.
2. Support systems should reflect customer's priorities. It is important to find out which service can be automated without losing the personal touch.
3. Getting feedback from the user is important to ascertain the quality of service. Regular users of an academic library can be given a questionnaire to get feedback from them for improving service.
4. The circulation desk staff are the front line staff who play a critical role is an academic library because they represent the library; first deal with inquiries/crises; manage the reader interface. Public services staff must be carefully appointed and be given periodic training to keep up-to-date.
5. All academic library staff must receive training, including skill training; on the job guidance; retraining. Well-trained staffs are the competitive weapons for better quality service in an academic library. Teamwork plays a vital role in giving better quality service. People have to develop a culture and commitment towards quality service in an academic library.
6. ISO 9000 Series Steps Towards TQM In Academic Library. ISO 9000 has an internationally accepted certificate that accredits an organization for its quality management systems and procedures. ISO 9004-2:1992 has guidelines for services and was issued by ISO to establish and implement a quality system within a service organization such as an educational institution.

10

Marketing of Information Products and Services for Libraries

A society that consumes and generates the most knowledge and information is the strongest society. The information industry has grown dramatically in services, revenue, and coherence over the last decade. Though the marketing of information services is a concept of comparatively recent origin, it has now emerged as an important area for libraries and information centers. Marketing covers those activities that connect the organization to those parts of its outside world that use, buy, sell or influence the outputs it produces and the benefits and services it offers (O'Shaughnessy). As Kotler points out, organizations such as museums, universities, libraries, and charities need to market their causes and their products to gain political and social support as well as economic support.

One of the major barriers to operating a profitable information business is the lack of business expertise among librarians and information scientists. Marketing is a comprehensive term that describes all the processes and interactions that result in satisfaction for users and revenue for the information firm. Libraries and information centers have begun to realize that marketing of information products and services is an integral part of administration, especially as a means for improving user satisfaction and promoting the use of services by current and potential users. Three main factors, namely the information explosion, the technology revolution, and escalating library costs are responsible for encouraging the library profession to develop a marketing approach in its operations and services. Some information service managers feel that marketing is inimical to the nature of their activities. But with increased competition in the world of information, marketing is a factor for survival. At the same time, there is a common misconception that promotional activities alone constitute marketing.

Information Management (IM)—IM is managing the processes of selection, collection building, processing, controlling, and dissemination of information in an organization. IM can help an organization recognize and use the potentials of the resources of information and information technology. (Brenner) Librarians have a significant role to play in IM. Considering the IM cycle, one can find that librarians have a role to play in almost every step in the information-user matching process.

Information Marketing

Basic Concepts and Definition: Marketing is planning and managing the organization's exchange relations with its clientele. It consists of studying the target market's needs, designing appropriate products and services, and using effective pricing, communication, and distribution to inform, motivate, and serve the market. The American Marketing Association defines marketing as those activities which direct the flow of goods and services, from production to consumption. The following are vital concepts

1. Marketing Activities

a. Market profiling is an important marketing activity, which is done to obtain marketing information. It is necessary to identify the market scope to formulate appropriate policies. Market profiling should consider:

- User affordability
- Extent of use
- Relevance of the service to users
- Repeat customers
- User preferences
- Staffing

b. Product planning is the marketing activity concerned with developing a product that satisfies customers. Management must decide:

- Who should be the user groups?
- To whom the information services/products should be targeted?
- What should be the services/products that can be produced and marketed to the different target groups?

c. Pricing is the marketing activity that determines the price of the product on the basis of costs as well as market factors such as distribution channels, discount structure, competitors' prices, ability or willingness of customers to pay, and so on. The following are questions to ask during pricing.

- What are the costs involved in the generation of services and products?
- What factors need to be considered in arriving at costs?
- Should the information services/products be given free? If so, to whom and why?
- What would be the impact in relation to the value of a product, if given free?
- What should be the criteria for pricing?

d. Promotion is the activity that covers all aids to sales. Promotion stimulates demand and increases sales. Usually promotion moves the product toward the customers. It involves mechanisms that inform the target groups about the resources available, services and products offered by the libraries/ information centers. Questions to ask regarding promotion:

- To whom is the promotional material directed?
- What is the message?
- What promotional mechanisms are available?
- What points are to be considered in the design of a promotional package?
- What is the role of the library staff in promotional activities?

e. Distribution is the marketing activity concerned with distributing the product from the manufacturer to the customer, making the product available and easy to buy. Following are the major channels of dissemination:

- Interpersonal delivery/Group personal delivery
- Strategic placement
- In-house dissemination
- Local depositories
- Mass media/Broadcasting

- Mail/Telephone/Computer network

2. Principles of Marketing Management

Modern library services should be based on the following marketing principles.

1. The company must have an active attitude towards the market. It cannot expect customers to buy a product simply because it is produced. The management must actively study the market, persuade customers, promote the product, and organize distribution.
2. Marketing should be given at least as much importance as other basic functions such as administration, production and finance.
3. The marketing function must be "integrated". This means that the various marketing considerations must be taken into account in the decisions of all the managers, not only those directly concerned with sales.

3. Marketing Techniques

Management is required to control the application of a range of skills and techniques in marketing, generally derived from practical industrial experience and from modern social sciences such as economics, statistics and applied psychology. Marketing skills and techniques can be divided into four broad groups.

- Those used in order to obtain data about the market
- Those used to create and stimulate demand
- Those used to analyze costs and other marketing factors
- Other practical skills and techniques

4. Marketing Strategy

Not all enterprises can afford to use all the marketing techniques. Furthermore, different situations require different techniques. The marketing manager must be able to select those techniques that are necessary for a particular product in a particular situation. Therefore, successful marketing includes the art of deciding which techniques to use in different situations. Marketing strategy also means selecting various techniques in proper proportion and balance.

5. Creating a Market

The proper and active use of marketing techniques provides

the possibility of creating a market. Here are three examples:

- Increasing the present volume of sales can create a market.
- Creating a market can mean waking up a sleeping market.
- Creating a market can involve creating a demand that did not exist at all.

Thus, the products are made and the market is created as a result of effective marketing strategy.

Professional Skills for Marketing: Library personnel require the following professional knowledge and skills for marketing information and library services:

- Perception of user needs and ability to obtain feedback from users
- Technical knowledge, such as ability to use the Internet
- Knowledge of various marketing strategies for promoting information skills

Factors which characterize the difficulties of marketing information services are:

- The relatively low level of knowledge and lack of agreement on user requirements, wants, and needs.
- The subsidized non-market environment in which most scientific and technical information products and services are used.
- The virtual impossibility of estimating the value contributed by information products and services to the efficiency and conduct of research and development and the advancement of scholarly pursuits
- The general economic unsophistication of those, mostly schooled in the humanities and the non-market-oriented library school environment, who purchase information products and services.

Hence the subjective concept of information makes marketing difficult. The value of information varies with the purpose and is also time and space dependent - hence, the difficulty in projecting the benefits of marketing information. There is also difficulty in estimating the contribution of information to R&D activity and to the advancement of scholarly pursuits. In addition, the reluctance of librarians and other information professionals to engage in marketing adds to the problems.

11

Marketing and Total Quality Management

Marketing and Total Quality Management (TQM) are closely and clearly interlinked. Marketing focuses on capturing and analysing customers' needs; TQM involves the question of whether products and services do correspond to customers' expectations and needs and whether both are congruent with each other. TQM has been defined as "a systematic process, which focuses on understanding customer needs and improving customer services" (Donald, 2003). The implementation of TQM in the Library is a useful way to evaluate the quality of library services and provide goals for improvement. One especially beneficial aspect of TQM is its emphasis on continuous improvement.

Libraries are both a creation and a servant of society. A library operates routinely with a known set of customers. A library also operates on trust. When a client walks into the library, he trusts that he will get the material or information that he needs. The library, in turn, trusts that the client will return the items within the specified borrowing period. The specific structure of a library with its strict requirements as to efficiency demands a focus on the quality of value-adding processes. If a library is to be managed according to quality criteria, quality needs to be defined and made measurable. The indicators found must be captured in a measuring system for the sectors "cost and performance", "customer satisfaction", and "staff satisfaction" that facilitates quality controlling and provides staff with controlling parameters for everyday work.

Concept of Marketing Library Services: The history of marketing library services began long before the concept was born. Samuel Swett Green in his often quoted speech at the ALA Conference in 1876 advocated "improved personal relations between librarians and readers." It could be said that today's marketing of library services has its roots in parts of the USA and Northern Europe, in countries with few illiterates and more money, libraries, and library schools than the rest of the world. This certainly does not mean that the idea of libraries reaching out to "the common man" has not occupied librarians in other parts of the world. For instance, there is the example of the "library movement" in India at the beginning of the 20th century (Renborg, 1997).

Basic Steps for Marketing Library and Information Services: Libraries and information centers of all types and sizes are faced with the need to market. Librarians and information professionals must learn to effectively market and advertise their services.

1. Competitions for customers—Libraries are part of a highly competitive service industry. Competition comes from mega-bookstores, online book dealers, consultants, the Internet, and individuals who feel they can go it alone. Libraries are no longer the only information show in town. Free web access to information is here to stay and non-library and fee access information providers won't hesitate to market to library customers.
2. Competition for resources—Libraries of all types have to compete with other organisations or departments for funds. Public libraries have to vie for public monies that provide for their existence. Special libraries find their funding is frequently targeted during parent organisation budget cuts. Marketing library services benefits the bottom line.
3. Maintain your relevance - Libraries need to market themselves to remain connected with their communities and have some bearing on real-world issues and present-day events.
4. Stop being taken for granted - Libraries need to convey what is unique about the access and services they provide. Both customers and librarians cannot assume that libraries will always be available.
5. Promote an updated image - Librarians are not perceived as well-trained, technologically savvy information experts.

Most customers do not see the demanding information management responsibilities of a librarian.

6. Visibility - Librarians are not on the radar screens of many people who think of themselves as information literate. People who are in positions to employ librarians are not reading much in their professional literature about a librarian's value.
7. Valuable community resource - Libraries are and should be viewed as essential and valuable community resources. People need to be made aware of the services and products that are provided and their comparative value. Librarians should be the resource that the local power structure goes to for information.
8. Rising expectations - Library users expect recognition, attention, and appreciation for their individual information needs. Customers also have ever-changing needs and wants, which makes the library market as dynamic as retail markets. Marketing helps to create an environment in libraries that fosters customer consciousness among employees.
9. Survival - Libraries depend on the support of others for their existence. A library must communicate and work with its customers and governing/funding entities to provide information about what the library is doing and to enable the library to learn about the community it serves.
10. Beneficial to library image - Effective marketing can among other things: increase library funds, increase usage of services, educate customers and non-customers, change perceptions, and enhance the clout and reputation of the library and its staff (Steadily, 2003).

Difficulties to Marketing Library and Information Services: Most librarians do not market their libraries, do not know how to market, or do not know how to do it well.

1. Old models - Many librarians work on the old model of existence by mandate.
   - Students should use library databases to locate quality information for their papers.
   - Faculty should send their students to librarians for assistance.

- Children should be brought to the library to learn about books.
- Middle managers should tap into the corporate library for information.

2. Humility-Too often librarians wait for others to notice that they are doing a good job. Librarians may be reluctant to capitalize on their strengths and knowledge, while the general public often does not see the value that information professionals could bring to sophisticated information challenges.
3. Myth-There is a belief that libraries do not need to be promoted in any special way because their importance to society should be apparent to all.
4. Old expectations-Librarians and libraries are limited by their traditional image; that libraries offer books for lending and provide programming for children, but do not contribute to more sophisticated information needs.
5. Lack of training and education-Often librarians do not promote library services well due to lack of training and knowledge of marketing tools and techniques. Although marketing is more widely discussed and accepted professionally than in the past, this acceptance hasn't necessarily resulted in more marketing classes in library schools' curricula. Despite the growing literature on library marketing, there remains a lack of familiarity with the total marketing concept among librarians.
6. Confusion-There is confusion about what the term marketing means. Much of this has to do with the interchangeability of terms such as 'promotion', 'public relations', 'publicity', and 'marketing'. There is also confusion about marketing libraries; the perception is that marketing is a business tool and not applicable to library settings.
7. Fear-Librarians are often reluctant to borrow from the private sector. They have a fear of commercial publicity and see marketing as manipulative, a waste of time and resources, and unprofessional.
8. Passive vs. active stance-Rather than selling the library on its value and letting people know what the Library and Information Center offers, librarians often wait for

customers to come to them. Rather than pushing out responses to anticipated information needs to customers, librarians wait for customers to stop by the facility or stumble across the library web site.

9. Complex and complicated task-Marketing is a complicated problem for libraries because of their wide range of products and services from books to Internet access, and an extremely diverse audience that ranges from children to seniors, public officials to business people, and students to faculty, etc.
10. Money and attitude-Lack of funds is often used as a reason or excuse not to market. However, marketing library services is not simply a matter of spending dollars on promotion and advertising. Marketing is also a matter of improving the customer's experience of library services. The attitude of the library director and the staff as they interact with customers is what shapes customers' experiences and 'markets' the library to those customers.

Relevance of Marketing for Librarians and Information Managers: To use the concept "marketing" librarians have brought over some management tools from the commercial world. That has been advantageous for the global library world. It has forced librarians to look at the libraries as the enterprises they are.

In the early conceptualisation of a Library and Information Centre's business, Dr. S. R. Ranganathan had the concept of customer orientation embedded into it. He described a library as..... a public institution or establishment charged with the care of a collection of books, the duty of making them accessible to those who require the use of them and the task of converting every person in its neighborhood into a habitual library into a habitual library user and reader of books.

SECTION II

OBJECTIVE/MULTIPLE TYPE QUESTIONS/ANSWERS

1

Information and Communication

1. What has Information Science Contributed to the World?

The following point has contributed by information to the society given by different information science researchers.

1. Information science researchers measured the information explosion. They created the field of bibliometrics—the study of published literature and its usage. Bibliometrics has many aspects, including studies of impact, diffusion of innovation, bibliographic coupling, citation and co-citation patterns and other statistical regularities in scientific and scholarly productivity and communication.
2. Information science developers contained the information explosion. Information scientists pioneered innovations in indexing systems that were very different from traditional subject cataloging in libraries—automatic indexing and abstracting, KWIC and KWOC indexing, citation indexing, keyword indexing and post coordination, text analysis and natural language searching systems. They also developed thesauri or controlled vocabularies for thousands of disciplines and specialties.
3. Information science developers applied computers to manipulating documents and document records in information storage and retrieval systems. This began almost as soon as computers became available in the 1950s, but really took off with third-generation computers in the 1960s. The development of online database systems was

accompanied by related telecommunications and networking technologies and specialized search functionalities, as well as large machine-readable databases. The application of formal logic (Boolean operators) to database searching was a major component of these developments.

4. Information science researchers studied users' information seeking, needs and preferences, as well as related areas such as relevance and utility assessment. The sociologists got us started, but we quickly developed our own body of research in the second half of the last century.
5. Information science leaders in government and industry contributed to formulating national information policies related to issues of privacy, security, regulating dissemination and access, intellectual property, acceptable use and others. They contributed to developing standards for the processing and communication of information, as well as the monitoring of the national information infrastructure (human, technological, materials and financial) to ensure that information systems and services related to the public interest were maintained.

2. What does Information Literacy Mean?

Information is a basic resource for all human beings and its importance is as good as food, air and water. Information literacy is the ability "to recognize when information is needed and have the ability to locate, evaluate and use effectively the needed information". An information literate person is one who:

- Recognizes that accurate and complete information is the basis for intelligent decision making
- Recognizes the need for information
- Formulates questions based on information needs
- Identifies potential sources of information
- Develops successful search strategies
- Accesses sources of information including computer-based and other technologies
- Evaluates information
- Organizes information for practical application
- Integrates new information into an existing body of knowledge

- Uses information in critical thinking and problem solving (Doyle, 1992)

Since information may be presented in a number of formats, the term information applies to more than just the printed word. Other literacies such as visual, media, computer, network, and basic literacies are implicit in information literacy.

3. What are the difference between Information, Knowledge, Wisdom and Leadership?

INFORMATION is simply data-raw material. It's like a news report that you listen to and passively absorb, but can't do anything about.

KNOWLEDGE is an understanding of information and requires work on your part. Knowledge places information in a broader context of things like history, processes, people, comparisons of data, and so on. Acquiring knowledge takes effort; you have to dig deeper into information to turn it into knowledge.

WISDOM goes one-step further- wisdom encompasses knowledge and what you do with your knowledge. One twist on wisdom, though, is that wisdom doesn't get anything done unless you choose to translate it into action. Wisdom requires personal effort to obtain but it involves no personal risk. Think of one of those political talk shows where the guest seems to know it all - there is a lot of wisdom being brought forward but very little risk because there is no action.

Finally, leadership is the application of wisdom for the purpose of achieving a goal. Leadership also involves change-as one responder to my question said, "Leadership is the act of influencing, in a wise, insightful manner, those around you to change-or make changes for the better." Leadership requires personal risk and involvement because it requires action; a leader is a doer, not an observer. Leadership is also situational and requires all of us to recognize who is the best-qualified person to deal with a situation. That person must step up and lead, and we must respect and support that person in his/her leadership role. A classic example is CPR and a heart attack victim. In a heart attack situation, the EMT or the person who knows CPR is the leader, not necessarily the highest-ranking manager on the scene.

4. Distinguish, among Knowledge, Information and Data

"Information" is "data" that has been processed. Data is raw facts and figures or unorganized pieces of information. Data became information when these pieces are processed, interpreted and presented in an organized or logical form to facilitate a better use, whereas Information is data that has been processed and given a context. On the other hand knowledge is the organized body of information . For example, a red traffic light is data. The meaning that we attach to this data is "Stop". When you drive up to a red light and stop, you do so because your brain sees the data and process it. Knowledge is an understanding of "rules". For example, "smoking can cause cancer", "revising hard means you stand a better chance of passing exams", "run and you will get there faster". A "knowledge worker" is someone who is employed because they understand rules related to a particular task.

The main difference between data and information is that: Data are raw isolated facts; information is data that is summarized or presented in a useful or meaningful way. Data are numbers; information is words or sentences. Data are inputted into computers; information can only be made by human beings. Data are always knowledge; information is never knowledge.

Knowledge as Power., organizations and individuals typically use information and knowledge to produce goods and services, solve problems, and exploit opportunities. The concept of knowledge as power is based on the idea that individuals and groups that possess information crucial to attaining organization goals have power. People in a position to control information about current operations, develop information about alternatives, or acquire knowledge about future events and plans, have enormous power to influence others.

5. What are the Value & Importance of Information?

Information is generated as a result of the different types of human activities, events or incidents. Activities are undertaken by individuals or by organizations to achieve specific objectives. Events are things that happen, occur or take place. Without activities or events there would be no information.

Its impo⁻tance can be more realized if it can reach to anybody anywhere in the globe without boundary. According to Kevin (1993), - "next to matter and energy information is all pervasive in this universe". It organizes, controls and runs any system, may be it biological, social or mechanical. It is the essence of communication – later was the lifeblood of any organism. At present information technology is fundamental to the success of any business. The information that is collected and/or assembled in any business is as valuable a resource as capital or people. Information may cover anything: market trends, buying preferences, customer profiles etc. It may be processed, summarised, and analysed by computers before being used by managers as the basis for decision-making. It is more than just the raw data from which it is derived, when it processed in a context then it became information and developed into something that is consumable by its users. It is only when these data are part of user processes that they can contribute to information. The abstract nature of these concepts makes it difficult to see a clear way to measure the impotence of information, even though there are established ways to quantify and characterize the associated data. Often a small amount of information will have greater value than large amounts if it used in a proper way in right time, thus there is no direct relationship between the quantity of data and the value of the associated information. Therefore, importance of information can be more when quality of data will be: accurate, up-to-date, complete and it can be reached to any body without limitations for a specific purpose in right time.

6. Explain the process of Information Communication?

In modern time, the information is treated as the strength and the important sources and base of the economic, social, industrial, educational and political development of a country. Explain the process of information communication. It is also treated as the base of the increasing development of the R & D programmes of the world. It may be utilized properly only when it should be sent or communicated to its users. To communicate, the information should be scripted and should be understandable. The process of communication of information may be divided into the following.

- The Communicator—The writer, poets, artists, lecturers, researchers etc are the agent of the communication system of information, who generate, communicate and transfer the information to the others.

- Message or information—What the communicator generates and disseminates, that is called the messages, which is also called information. It should be clear, simple and understandable.
- Transmission—The communicator of information transmits the message or information through a book, article, lecture, radio/TV/film display etc. which are called sources or media. Thus the communication, transmission and flow of the information come in the forms of publication, reproduction and indexing of documents. Here the process of information is completed.
- Receiver—The message of the information generated by the communicator is transferred by the media and receiver receive the same. In this way who receive the information is called the receiver.

7. Describe the barriers in Information Communication?

In the information process, there have been so many operations. In these operations some difficulties may occur naturally in the free flow of the information, which are called the barriers of communication. There are some common barriers –

- Foreign languages
- Economic problems
- Political problems
- Time log
- Procedures
- Lack of manpower
- Lack of cooperation

8. What is Information and Communications Technology (ICT)?

Technology is the application of science to everyday tasks. Information and Communications Technology is the application of science to:

- Collecting data
- Storing data
- Processing/manipulating data
- Transferring data
- Outputting information

9. Whether the Librarianship is a Profession?

The profession is called occupation also and meaning of the profession is to those operations, which are executed either in the factory or at home with the help of other workers. The service occupations are those in which a man earns the money be serving the others or by selling his services to them. Example- the professions of lawyers, doctors, teachers and librarians are counted in this category. These people earn money by selling their services to others. In this way the profession concerned with librarianship falls under the category of utilitarianistic profession. These are some affirmative points for librarians as profession.

- Libraries of today are not only the storehouse of books but also are the analysis centers of information.
- Today libraries needs more experienced, skilful and technically expert personals.
- The librarian handles different types of users by his different abilities and efficiencies and satisfies their information needs.
- Present trends marketing of information also directly sell its information
- Information consultancy, interlibrary loan, resource sharing, browsing of network etc also involved with financial activities of library

10. Describe the Main Functions of a Library Association?

The meaning of the word association is to remain collectively in a group of persons/institutions working together for some objectives. In context of libraries, the association means the organization of library staff members. So the library association is an institution of persons or organizations related with the library jobs and profession This may be local, regional state, national and international levels.

Functions of Library Associations:

1. Planning for library, lib. staff and lib. Services.
2. To establish a strong organization
3. Brotherhood in library professionals
4. Awaking of reading habits in the society
5. Passing of library act
6. Organizing seminars, conferences, workshops and comps on library topics

7. To prepare moral rules codes of conduct for the librarian
8. To establish uniformity/standards effectiveness among libraries
9. Training for library staff
10. Relation and cooperation's with other/equivalent associations

2

Information and Reference Source/Services

11. Differentiate between Reference Service and Information Service?

Reference service (RS) is the ultimate goal of all library services. It is the service that connects the users with their document and information needs and helps the processing of promoting use of the collections built up in a library. It is personalized service offered to users. On the other hand Information service (IS) mean to inform its users on any required information as it is published. It is retrospective searching which is concerned with provision of answers to a specific enquires.

- RS refers to the traditional approach as Ranganathans Five Laws of library science, but IS is to provide information itself, which is based on up-to-date method.
- In RS the user is directed to the tools containing information, he is expected to locate information himself, but in IS an attempt is to provide information pin-pointedly, exhaustively and expeditiously.
- RS concerned with the provision of information on

demand/ specific quarries, but IS lays emphasis on providing information in anticipation of demand for it and the staff does not wait for the users but goes ahead with the job, the aim ias to assist the user to keep up-to-date in his field.

12. What is the Importance of National Bibliography?

Bibliography is a useful tool for study and research. A national bibliography is the publications of a nation as a whole. Example: INB (India) , BNB (UK) , ANB (Australia) etc.

- The importance of national bibliography for a country cannot be overstated. At one level it is a permanent cultural and documentary record of a country's publications recording the accumulated knowledge, activities and achievements of its citizens in all fields of human endeavour.
- National bibliographies aid libraries in the selection and acquisition of new materials and serve as current awareness and reference sources for librarians, researchers and bibliographers.
- The bibliographic records which constitute the national bibliography are a basis for the achievement of Universal Bibliographic Control which has the aim of making "universally and promptly available, in a form which is internationally acceptable, basic bibliographic data on all publications issued in all countries".
- It is very valuable tool for book selection, classification and cataloguing work for the libraries
- It is a guide to book vender/ suppliers/ publishers etc.

13. How do you evaluate Indian National Bibliography?

A. Detail and Description:

- Name- INB
- First Edition- 1957
- Nature – It is Current/unto date
- Kind- It is INB of India

B. Authority:

- Central Reference Library housed in the National Library, Kolkatta

C. Scope/ Area:

- Publications—books, periodicals, newspapers, maps/ atlas, etc.
- Languages—published literature of 16 registered languages
  - Script—Roman and English
  - Arrangement—two parts (General & Govt. Pub.) classified and alphabetical
- Treatment—publication periodicity (Quartely-upto 1964, Monthly)

D. Other Features/Drawbacks:

- It is significant
- It is very irregular
- It fails to be comprehensive
- There is no provision of penalties in "Delivery of Books Act of India", so many publications are not included in it. Now many electronics publications are not included.

14. How Computer Based CAS/SDI is Provided?

Human nature is ever keen to keep abreast of new development in his field, so he needs his current approach to information. Any service intended to meet this current approach is generally known as Current Awareness Service (CAS). The most important characteristic of CAS is speed of information availability. CAS appears in various forms like – Information Bulletin in regular intervals on a week/fortnightly/monthly through manual/ electronic mail, Title announcement, Content list, Indexing and Abstracting services etc. The components of CAS Bulletin: a) A bibliographic citation consisting – author/title/locus of document, b) On the basis of subject heading , alphabetically and c) A list of address of authors on a specific subject etc.

- The following techniques are specified for providing CAS:
- Telephone calls to the individual
- Recording individual references and forwarding them
- Periodical routing
- Maintaining files of references of information
- Issuing of library bulletin
- Circulation of duplicated contents of periodicals

On the other hand, Selective Dissemination of Information (SDI) was developed with a specific purpose of providing a researcher at regular intervals a carefully selected list of all publications in his particular areas of interest that have been published in the world. Once the policy aspects associated with the design of an SDI system are decided by the concerned authority, then appropriate decision of its components are taken. The next stage is to organize the SDI system step by step and operate it. The essential steps needed for this purpose are:

- *Document Profile:* Creation of Database-selection of appropriate bibliographical information for the database, input preparation, preparation of searchable file.
- *Construction of Users Search Profile:* It is a list of terms used for describing the user's query based on his field of interest in a narrative way.
- *Searching for IRS (Inf. Retrieval System)/Search Profile:* the information scientist constructs the search profile by selecting the search terms from thesaurus and other reference tools.
- *Matching:* with the contents of the databases with the search terms in search profile.
- *Notification:* After matching the search result to be notified to the user

15. Distinguish, between POPSI and PRECIS

In the field of subject indexing, PRECIS (PREserved Context Indexing System developed by Derek Austin during 1970) and POPSI (Postulated based Permuted Subject Indexing developed by Gonesh Bhattacharya of DRTC) are most important (pre-coordinate) indexing systems which are the developed version of Chain Indexing (SR Ranganathan) Both these indexing systems largely based on classificatory principles which fix the citation order of concepts and the network of selected concepts with reference to any given concept.

Both are helpful in deriving the subject heading and subject index entries in a consistent way. The format and structure are based on postulates and principles in POPSI and role operators in PRECIS regulate the writing of input strings.

In PRECIS as a system in which the initial strings of terms organized according to a scheme of role indicating operator, it is designed for computer manipulation and based on principle of classification. But POPSI is based on some fundamental theoretical ideas not based on any particular system of classification.

The format of component terms in PRESIS consists some what of a one-toone,i.e. a hierarchical relationship, while in POPSI the relationship is based on certain postulates and principles like – A.B.C.D.

16. What are the qualities of a Good Abstract?

It is the bibliographical detail/ brief statement of an current original research output/article. It acts as retrieval media and as current awareness tool

Qualities of a good abstract:

- Brief in size
- Express the basic aim and conclusion of the document
- Accurate to its title
- Clear in style of writing
- It should be with the rule, method and technique

Principles:

1. Ranganthan Says an abstract should be-
   - Positive Principle—short, up-to-date, new techniques, important data
   - Negative Principle—Original title of the article, well known authors information, full sentences etc should not be included and telegraphic language should be used.
2. Size: Standard size, 50-150 words, the best is , 200-250 words
3. Wording: It should be in proper order and economy of word to be maintained.
4. Sentences: brief with full meaning.
5. Labguage: easy and simple, use of slant language/ symbols/trade names to be avoided.
6. Style of writing: to be in past tense and conclusion to be in present tence.

Examples

- Chemical Abstract, Ohio, USA, Biological Abstract, BIOSIS, USA.
- Indian Science Abstract, New Delhi, India

17. What is a Database? Explain the structure and Features of MARC–II?

Database is an organized set of data stored in a computer and which can be searched automatically. Database contains usable raw data or a description of the sources where data can be found. It generally refers a machine-readable file in a systematic way, which generally embodies in the magnetic tape or disk of a computer or bibliographical records but may be use more specifically to refer to a shared collection of structured data managed by a set of special software. This may be bibliographic and non-bibliographic database

Library of Congress (LC) started a Pilot Project in 1966 to provide data for Machine Readable Catalogue (MARC) after 2 year it stopped and then MARC-II was started. A library can get the machine-readable catalogue data in the form of magnetic tape, in which the descriptions of American and foreign publications are contained.

Structure of MARC-II

LEEDER (24 character)-RECORD DIRECTORY (12 character)-VARIABLE FIELDS

Leader provides information on–total length, type and bibliographical level of record. Record Directory provides variable fields and their location in the record.

Features:

- The organization of cataloguing of document in it is done by a central committee.
- Include-books, journal's, film, maps, atlases etc.
- It provides copies of magnetic tapes
- Catalogue in the card forms also printed Prepare cumulative volumes and printed card
- BNB is also using it with the help of LC.
- It can available in online form
- Used for bibliographical control at international level.

3

Information Processing and Organisation/Retrieval

18. What is a Library Catalog? How, it Serves the Purpose of the User?

A library catalog (or library catalogue) is a register of all bibliographic items found in a library. A bibliographic item can be any information entity (e.g., books, computer files, graphics, relia, cartographic materials, etc.), that is considered library material (e.g., a single novel in an anthology), or a group of library materials (e.g., a trilogy), or linked from the catalog (e.g., a webpage) as far as it is relevant to the catalog and to the users (patrons) of the library.

Goal of a library catalog.: A library catalog typically serves to answer the following questions:

- Does the library have a specific work?
- Which works by a particular author does the library have?
- Which works about a particular subject does the library have?
- Which works a particular author has written?
- Which works about a particular subject have been published?

In addition, a catalog may serve internal purposes of the library, for example as an inventory of everything that should be present.

19. What are the types of Library Catalogue

Traditionally, there are the following types of catalog:

- Author catalog: a formal catalog, sorted alphabetically according to the authors' or editors' names of the entries.
- Title catalog: a formal catalog, sorted alphabetically according to the title of the entries.
- Keyword catalog: a subject catalog, sorted alphabetically according to some system of keywords.
- Mixed alphabetic catalog forms: sometimes, one finds a mixed author/title, or an author/title /keyword catalog.
- Systematic catalog: a subject catalog, sorted according to some systematic subdivision of subjects.

Shelf list catalog: a formal catalog with entries sorted in the same order as bibliographic items are shelved.

20. Discuss about, Library Catalogue and it's various Rules?

Library catalogs originated as manuscript lists, arranged by format (folio, quarto, etc.) or in a rough alphabetical arrangement by author. Printed catalogs enabled scholars outside a library to gain an idea of its contents. These would sometimes be interleaved with blank leaves on which additions could be recorded, or bound as guard books in which slips of paper were bound in for new entries. The first card catalogs appeared in the nineteenth century, enabling much more flexibility, and towards the end of the twentieth century the OPAC was developed (see below). 1595: Nomenclature of Leiden University Library appears, the first printed catalog of an institutional library.

Cataloging rules- Cataloging rules have been defined to allow for consistent cataloging of various library materials across several persons of a cataloging team and across time. Users can use them to clarify how to find an entry and how to interpret the data in an entry. Cataloging rules prescribe

- Which information from a bibliographic item is included in the entry;
- How this information is presented on a catalog card or in a cataloging record;
- How the entries should be sorted in the catalog.

The larger a collection, the more elaborate cataloging rules are needed. Users cannot and do not want to examine hundreds of catalog entries or even dozens of library items to find the one item they need. Currently, most cataloging rules are similar to, or even based on, the International Standard Bibliographic Description (ISBD), a set of rules produced by the International Federation of Library Associations (IFLA) to describe a wide range of library materials. These rules organize the bibliographic description of an item in the following areas: title and statement of responsibility (author or editor), edition, material-dependent information (for example, the scale of a map), publication and distribution, physical description (for example, number of pages), series, note, and standard number (ISBN). Library items that are written in a foreign script are, in some cases, transliterated to the script of the catalog.

21. What is Library Classification?

A library classification is a system of coding and organizing library materials (books, serials, audiovisual materials, computer files, maps, manuscripts, reels) according to their subject. A classification consists of tables of subject headings and classification schedules used to assign a class number to each item being classified, based on that item's subject.

Until the 19th century, most libraries had closed stacks, so the library classification only served to organize the subject catalog. In the 20th century, libraries opened their stacks to the public and started to shelve the library material itself according to some library classification to simplify subject browsing. There are many standard systems of library classification in use, and many more have been proposed over the years. These include:

- Library of Congress classification (LC)
- Dewey Decimal Classification (DDC) (mostly used in the English-speaking world.)
- Bliss bibliographic classification
- Colon classification
- Cutter Expansive Classification
- Universal Decimal Classification
- Brinkler classification

22. Discuss, Major types of Classification Schemes?

There are four major types of classification schemes: CC, LCC/ LCSH, UDC, and DDC etc.

Colon Classification: Colon Classification is the first example of an analytico-synthetic system, in which the subject field is first analysed into facets, and class numbers are then constructed by synthesis. For Ranganathan, the problem with the DDC and LCC schemes was that they used terms that had to be figured out before the item being described could fit into the scheme. With the explosion of information in the early 20th Century, the enumerative systems could not keep up. Ranganathan's solution was the development of facets, which allows for greater flexibility in addition to a high degree of specificity. Ranganathan developed five fundamental facets: Personality, Matter, Energy, Space, and Time (PMEST).

- Personality—what the object is primarily "about". This is considered the "main facet".
- Matter—the material of the object.
- Energy—the processes or activities that take place in relation to the object.
- Space—where the object happens or exists.
- Time—when the object occurs.

Ranganathan believed that any concept could be represented by pulling relevant pieces from these five facets and fitting them together. All of the facets do not need to be represented, and each can be used any number of times. The notation for each facet was separated by a colon, hence the name of the system. Colon Classification is general rather than specific in nature. Through the use of facets, it can create complex or new categories. It has main and generalized classes represented by a mixed notation of Arabic numerals, and Roman and Greek letters. In addition, there are four floating tables that correspond to subdivisions such as form, geography, time, and language.

Library of Congress Classification and Subject Headings (LCC/LCSH): "One of the world's most widely spread classification schemes is the Library of Congress Classification System (LCC). This is largely due to the fact that every exported record from the Library of Congress contains their own classification of the item. Apart from being dominating, it is quite old: LCC will soon celebrate its centenary. In 1899 the Librarian of Congress Dr. Herbert Putnam and his Chief Cataloguer Charles Martel decided to start a new classification system for the collections of the Library of Congress (established 1800). Basic features were taken from Charles Ammi Cutter's Expansive

Classification. LCC is an enumerative system built on 21 major classes, each class being given an arbitrary capital letter between A-Z, with 5 exceptions: I, O, W, X, Y (these appear at the second or third level in the notation for various subclasses). After this was decided, Putnam delegated the further development of different parts of the system to subject specialists, cataloguers and classifiers. Initially and intentionally the system was, and has remained, decentralised and the different classes and subclasses were published for the first time between 1899-1940. This has lead to the fact that schedules often differ very much in number and the kinds of revisions accomplished." [From the DESIRE Report]

Library of Congress Classification System. An outline of the LC system. "The Library of Congress Classification System (LC System) is used to organize books in many academic and university libraries throughout the United States and world. The LC System organizes material in libraries according to twenty-one branches of knowledge. The 21 categories (labeled A-Z except I,O,W,X and Y) are further divided by adding one or two additional letters and a set of numbers. ... This outline which is part of the Geography site at The Mining Company"

Dewey Decimal Classification (DDC): "The Dewey Decimal Classification System (DCC) was first produced by Melvil Dewey in 1876, originally being produced for a small North American college library. It is currently in its 21st edition (Mitchell 1995; Mitchell, et al. 1996) and is published by Forest Press. DDC is distributed in Machine-Readable Cataloguing (MARC) records produced by the Library of Congress (LC) and bibliographic utilities like OCLC and RLIN. DDC is also used in the national bibliographies of the UK, Canada, Australia, Italy and other countries (Comaromi, et al. 1990, p.6). Research carried out by OCLC in the 1980s established that DDC was a suitable tool for browsing, first for library catalogues and then for the Internet." [from the DESIRE Report]

"Both UDC and DDC are enumerative schemes and have a hierarchical structure that provide a systematic arrangement of subjects. Both schemes go beyond a strictly enumerative structure by the use of symbols (auxiliary tables) to enable compound subjects to be built (however this facility is not currently used by either of the services). There are many similarities between the notations of the two schemes (the UDC was originally adapted from the DDC scheme)..."

Scorpion "Scorpion is a project of the OCLC Office of Research exploring the indexing and cataloging of electronic resources. Since subject information is key to advanced retrieval, browsing, and clustering, the primary focus of Scorpion is the building of tools for automatic subject recognition based on well-known schemes like the Dewey Decimal System. ... OCLC has initiated the Scorpion research project to address the challenge of applying classification schemes and subject headings cost effectively to electronic information. A thesis of Scorpion is that the Dewey Decimal Classification can be used to perform automatic subject assignment for electronic item... The Dewey decimal classification is the most widely used classification scheme in the world. Currently, it is used in 135 countries and has been translated into 30 languages. In the United States it is used in 95% of all public and school libraries, and a large number of college, university, and special libraries. First published in 1876, it has been continuously revised to meet evolving information access needs both in the traditional library and in the electronic environments. It is currently in its 21st edition. Dewey is a hierarchical classification scheme. Each concept is denoted by a number that concisely identifies it and indicates its position in the hierarchy. For readability Dewey numbers are presented with a minimum length of three. Dewey numbers longer than three have a decimal point after the first three digits. The first digit (hundreds) represents the major disciplines; the second digit (tens) represents sub-disciplines of the hundreds; the third digit (ones) represents sub-disciplines of the tens, and so forth. Each number is significant. Generally, a longer number represents a more specific concept, and a shorter number represents a more general concept..."See http://www.oclc.org/research/software/scorpion/default.htm

Universal Decimal Classification (UDC): "The UDC is a general classification scheme of over 60,000 classes as well as a number of auxiliary tables used to describe countries, areas, etc.""The Universal Decimal Classification (UDC) is an international scheme which endeavours to cover all areas of knowledge. Its origins lie in the Dewey Decimal Classification (DDC), which was adapted towards the end of the Nineteenth century by Paul Otlet and Henri LaFontaine in an attempt to create a universal bibliography. Until recently responsibility for the scheme belonged to the FID (Federation Internationale de Documentation), this responsibility was passed to a consortium of publishers (the UDC Consortium) in 1992. The original purpose of use for ordering and indexing entries in a printed bibliography have since been overtaken by its use for indexing and retrieval in computer based systems. The scheme consists of 60,000 classes (divisions and sub-divisions) as well as a number of auxiliary tables to describe countries, etc." [From the DESIRE Report]

Note: "SOSIG uses the UDC (Universal Decimal Classification) scheme to create the browsing sections of the service. It was originally chosen in order to co-operate with other UK based Internet gateways and because there was no suitably broad social science classification scheme available. SOSIG does not use the UDC in its complete form, but has drawn upon a selection of over 160 UDC numbers pertaining to the social sciences from the scheme." See http://www.sosig.ac.uk/

IFLA Section on Classification and Indexing: IFLA Section on Classification and Indexing. Principles Underlying Subject Heading Languages (SHLs), being "a culmination of several years' work by the Working Group on Principles Underlying Subject Heading Languages, was published in August 1999. The work was completed under the editorship of Maria Ines Lopes of Portugal and Julianne Beall of the United States. See http://www.ifla.org/VII/s29/index.htm. For Different Questions related on classification see also the website http://www.lub.lu.se/desire/handbook/class.html

23. Discuss, different types of Classification Systems?

There are the following classification systems-

- Enumerative: produce an alphabetical list of subject headings, assign numbers to each heading in alphabetical order
- Hierarchical: divides subjects hierarchically, from most general to most specific
- Faceted or analytico-synthetic: divides subjects into mutually exclusive orthogonal facets

The most common classification systems, LC and DDC, are essentially enumerative, though with some hierarchal and faceted elements, especially at the broadest and most general level. The first true faceted system was the Colon classification of S. R. Ranganathan.

24. What is Subject Classification?

Subject classification is a method of describing resources by their subject and a means of organising knowledge in libraries and other information environments. Universal classification schemes designed for use by libraries began to be developed in North America during the nineteenth century. For example, the most famous (and most widely used) scheme is the Dewey Decimal Classification (DDC) system that was first produced for a small college library in 1876.

Classification schemes differ from other subject indexing systems (subject headings, thesauri, etc.) by trying to create collections of related resources in a hierarchical structure. The use of notations/codes facilitates the creation of hierarchical subject trees. For example, using UDC we can create the following hierarchy (adapted from: McIlwaine, 1995, p. 17:

5	Natural sciences
504	Environmental science
504.05	Adverse effects of human activity on the environment
504.054	Effect of harmful materials. Pollution
504.054(44)	The effect of pollution on the environment in France

Libraries have long experience of applying classification schemes to resources - chiefly books. The idea of classification is to make it easier for users to find and retrieve resources. By building a hierarchical structure, a classification scheme enables users to look for related items that have not previously been identified as relevant. This facilitates browsing - both within a physical library or online.

25. What are the Objective of OCLC

Founded in 1967, and originally named Ohio Computer Library Center, OCLC Online Computer Library Center is a nonprofit, membership, computer library service and research organization dedicated to the public purposes of furthering access to the world's information and reducing information costs. More than 50,000 libraries in 84 countries and territories around the world use OCLC services to locate, acquire, catalog, lend and preserve library materials. It is located in Columbus, Ohio.

Researchers, students, faculty, scholars, professional librarians and other information seekers use OCLC services to obtain bibliographic, abstract and full-text information when and where they need it. OCLC and its member libraries cooperatively produce and maintain WorldCat—the OCLC Online Union Catalog, the largest OPAC in the world. WorldCat contains holding records from most public and private libraries worldwide. WorldCat is available through many libraries and university computer networks.

The Open WorldCat program makes records of library-owned materials in OCLC's WorldCat database available to Web users on popular Internet search, bibliographic and bookselling sites. OCLC member libraries' catalogs are more accessible from the sites where many people start their search for information.

26. What is an On-line Catalog? How, can we Search with an OPAC

On-line cataloging has greatly enhanced the usability of catalogs. The on-line catalog does not need to be sorted statically; the user can choose author, title, keyword, or systematic order dynamically. Most on-line catalogs offer a search facility for any word of the title; the goal of the grammatic word order (provide an entry on the word that most users would look for) is reached even better. Many on-line catalogs allow links between several variants of an author name. So, authors can be found both under the original and the standardised name (if entered properly by the cataloger).

Searching with an OPAC- The acronym OPAC means Online Public Access Catalog. Many libraries have their book catalog accessible via Internet; some of them can be queried using a simple browser, other using a special version of browser (with JavaScript and CSS features), some others using Z39.50 clients. If you are looking for a book, you can access to the OPAC of your nearest library and search for it there.

If you want to look if a book exists and you have few elements to identify it, you can use a meta-searcher: you can fill the query form once and spread you search over many library catalogues. A service such as MultiOpac does this task for you. External links - A general overview of the ISBD (http://www.ifla.org/VII/s13/pubs/isbdg.htm)

27. Discuss about AACR-II

AACR2 stands for the Anglo-American Cataloging Rules, Second Edition. It is published jointly by the American Library Association, the Canadian Library Association, and the Chartered Institute of Library and Information Professionals. AACR2 is designed for use in the construction of catalogs and other lists in general libraries of all sizes. The rules cover the description of, and the provision of access points for, all library materials commonly collected at the present time.

Despite the claim to be 'Anglo-American', the first edition of AACR was published in 1967 in somewhat distinct North American and British texts. The second edition of 1978 unified the two sets of rules (adopting the British spelling 'cataloguing') and brought them in line with the International Standard Bibliographic Description. Libraries wishing to migrate from the previous North American text were obliged to implement 'desuperimposition', a substantial change in the form of headings for corporate bodies.

Principles of AACR include cataloguing from the item 'in hand' rather than inferring information from external sources and the concept of the 'chief source of information' which is preferred where conflicts exist. As well as occasional minor amendments, a broader revision is under way with a view to a new edition in which the rules are more consistent and coherent, informed by the Functional Requirements for Bibliographic Records. This 'AACR3' has the working title 'Resource Description and Access'.

28. What are the Coverage of Chemical Abstract

CA is published weekly, and there are 26 weekly issues per "volume". There are two volumes per year. Each Abstract issue is divided into 80 Subject Sections. Each abstract appears in just one section, based on the novelty of the process or substance being reported in the literature. Each weekly issue contains indexes by author, subject keyword (not official headings), and patent number. Individual issue indexes are superseded first by a volume index published every six months, and then by the Collective Index. Available in print, microform, and CD-ROM.

Coverage- CA content has always included the chemical aspects of a variety of scientific disciplines. An annual subscription to CA provides you with more than 814,000 references to the published literature each year. This consists of more than:

- 645,000 document references linked to the latest findings from 9,500 major scientific journals
- 345,000 patent equivalent references from 50 active patent-issuing authorities around the world
- Content: 52 Weekly Abstract Issues a year containing- CA abstracts from both journal articles and patents, index terms from three Weekly Indexes - Author Index, - Keyword Index, - Patent Index. —Two sets of five Volume Indexes (one set every 6 months) - Author Index , Patent Index , General Subject Index , Chemical Substance Index , Formula Index

CAS chemists create abstracts from:- journal articles, chemical and chemical engineering patents, technical reports, dissertations, conference proceedings and books . Each abstract contains:- complete bibliographic references , patent references (details of what was patented by whom and the country in which the patent was issued) , commonly used chemical substance names or molecular formulas , chemical structure images (when available) . Three indexes arrive weekly with the CA abstract issues:

- Author Index - an alphabetical listing of authors, inventors, patent assignees, and corporate author names.
- Keyword Index - an alphabetical listing of words and phrases taken from the title or text of the abstract.
- Patent Index - a list of all patent numbers that have been abstracted in the issue, along with the abstract number.

29. What are the Types of CA Volume Indexes

There are six major types of chemical index:

1. *Author Index*—This is an alphabetical listing of names of authors, coauthors, inventors, and patent assignees linked to the CA abstract number. Both personal and corporate names are included. The name of the first author is linked with the title of the original document or patent. Coauthors are cross-referred to the name of the first author.
2. *Patent Index*—An alphabetical listing of patent offices. Within the listing for each country, patents are arranged in ascending numerical order. Each patent number is followed by either—a CA abstract number and a complete

history of all equivalent documents .or a cross-reference to the patent number of the first abstracted patent in the patent family.

3. *General Subject Index*—This index links subject terms, such as reactions, classes of substances, and plant and animal species, with their corresponding CA abstract numbers. Most entries include a text-modification phrase, which further describes aspects of the topic covered in the original document.
4. *Chemical Substance Index*—This index consists of an alphabetical listing of CA index names—each of which identifies a specific chemical substance—linked to their appropriate abstract numbers. CAS Registry Numbers® are provided with this index. Entries also include the text-modification phrases that describe certain aspects of the substances that were studied.
5. *Formula Index*—An index of chemical substances that links molecular formulas with their CA index names, CAS Registry Numbers, and CA abstract numbers.

CA Index Guide—For the Fifteenth Collective Index (15CI) Period (2002-2006), the complete Index Guide (including Appendices) will be reissued three times. This reference, included as part of your CA subscription,

- Helps you search the Chemical Substance and the General Subject Indexes more effectively
- Links the substance names and subject terms that authors use in the published literature with the controlled terminology of the CA Volume Indexes
- Provides useful terms for searching online in the CAS databases

30. Give us the Current Subscription information of CA

2005 CA print, microform, and CA on CD Prices- $27,200 Full-Service CA Print , $27,200 on Microfilm , $30,200* on CD . Shipping and handling charges - $2,820 Elsewhere outside U.S. 2005 Subscription information - 52 Weekly Abstract Issues of CA Number of books , Volume 142: January-June, weekly abstracts and indexes -26 books , Volume 143: July-December, weekly abstracts and indexes- 26 books , 6-month Volume Indexes Number of books, Volume 142: January-June 30 books* , Volume 143: July-

December 30 books* ,TOTAL NUMBER OF BOOKS 112 books* .CA is available in a variety of formats - Print 214 books* , Microform (microfiche - 105mm x 148mm), Volume Indexes available in print only , 52 issues of fiche , microfilm (16mm reels with labels) - Kodak Ektamate magazines, - 3M cartridges,Volume Indexes available in print only 96 reels of film CA on CD - 8 discs . list of resources available on http://www.cas.org/PRINTED/caresources.html

Collective Index - Every five years CAS publishes a Collective Index (CI), which gathers and revises all the semi-annual indexes for the previous 5-year CI period. The 14th CI was published in 2002 and covers the years 1997-2001.

- In 1957 the indexing period was changed from 10 years (decennial) to five years (collective).
- The Subject Index was subdivided into the General Subject and Chemical Substance Indexes beginning with the 9th Collective Index period.
- 27-year Collective Formula Index (1920-1946).
- In 1981 the Numerical Patent Index and Patent Concordance were merged into the Patent Index.
- The Ring Systems Index was discontinued after the 12th Collective Index period.

31. What is an Indexing System

An index is a specific kind of tool for finding information. Whether an index is used by a human being or by a machine, its essence is a list of index entries. Each index entry leads to an indexed item somewhere outside the index; for instance, to a record in a database, to a folder in a file drawer, or a book on a library shelf. The entries are in some recognizable order, usually alphabetical. A back-of-the book index is alphabetical by subject and points to a page number(s) in the work with information about that subject:. Example- HITCHCOCK, ALFRED JOSEPH 14, this entry tells the user that there is information about Alfred Hitchcock on page 14 of the book.

32. What are Citation Indexes?

Citation indexes track references that authors put in the bibliographies of published papers. They provide a way to search for and analyze the literature in a way not possible through simple keyword/topical searching. It also enables users to gather data on the "performance" of individual authors and journals, as well as assessing particular areas of research activity and publication. This latter work is called bibliometrics.

Citation indexing began in the 1950s, and the market is controlled by the Institute for Scientific Information in Philadelphia, creator and publisher of the three citation indexes available today: Science Citation Index (SCI), Social Sciences Citation Index (SSCI), and Arts & Humanities Citation Index (AHCI). Remarks below focus on the use of SCI in the "hard" sciences, which have the longest track record in citation studies. All three ISI citation indexes are available online to UT users via the Web of Science system. UT has licensed ISI data back to 1975.

33. Why Use Citation Indexes?

1. *Find papers that cite earlier papers:* Citation indexing is a way to look forward in the literature from the starting point of a particular paper or group of papers. This is a different and complementary approach to ordinary word-based literature searching, which looks backward in the literature from the present time. For example, if you have an excellent paper on a particular topic that was published in 1992, you can use Science Citation Index (via Web of Science) to find papers published after 1992 that cited that paper. Citation implies a direct subject relationship between the papers. So, by searching for later papers citing your known paper, you can find more documents on the same or similar topic without using keywords or subject terms at all.

2. *Find out how many times my papers has been cited:* Science Citation Index is the only way to do this, but you must be aware up front that the data can be fuzzy, incomplete, and misleading at times. If you need to know the number of citations you've received for promotion and tenure purposes, you should exercise EXTREME CAUTION in gathering and interpreting this data. It is best to consult a librarian or citation expert before doing this kind of analysis. It can be very time-consuming, and the risk of undercounting is high. You don't want personnel decisions to depend on it.

3. *See which are the best journals in my field:* Citation data have long been used to rank journals within particular subject fields, usually based on the ISI Impact Factor. The impact factor is simply

a numerical ratio of the total number of citations a given journal receives in one year to the total number of articles it published in the previous two years. It is a useful way to see how journals perform in relation to others in the same subject area. It is NOT particularly useful in comparing journals across subject areas.

For example, Journal A has an impact factor of 4.327, and Journal B has an impact factor of 1.045. Is Journal A "better" than Journal B? You could make that argument, if both A and B are in the same basic field, such as Analytical Chemistry or Spectroscopy. But if A is in Biochemistry, and B is in Clinical Pharmacy, no such judgment can be made. Citation behavior varies considerably from field to field. Thus, impact factors are only meaningful in context with other journals in the same field. An editor might say, "My journal has an impact factor of 3.254 this year." That means nothing by itself. He would rather say, "My journal ranked 2nd out of 38 journals in its subject category this year."

Impact factors for journals covered by ISI are published annually in an electronic compilation called Journal Citation Reports. The Science Edition of the JCR is available to UT users on the web. All ISI Source Journals are ranked within one or more relevant subject categories, such as CHEMISTRY, ORGANIC or SPECTROSCOPY. JCR also contains data on historical trends, immediacy index, cited half-life, etc.

4. Decide which journal to submit my articles to: The same concepts apply to your decision to submit your articles to one journal or another. You would like to get it published in the "best" journal in your field, so that it will be read and cited. Examining relative impact factors is a good way to start. But your decision should also take into account other factors, such as publication turnaround time, likelihood of acceptance, type of paper (letter, review, full paper, etc.), subject scope and relevance, size of audience, as well as factors like subscription cost and editorial policies. Impact factor ranking is just one part of the equation, but it's the best available numerical rating for journals today.

5. Verify old and obscure references: Sometimes you'll find a reference in a paper to a very old or strange article or book, and you won't be able to figure out what it's referring to. By searching that reference as a "cited reference" in Web of Science, sometimes you can find other, more complete citations that might solve the mystery. It doesn't matter how old the mystery paper is — if someone has cited it since 1975 it will show up in the Citation Index.

34. Discuss about Science Citation Index

Science Citation Index (SCI) provides access to current and retrospective bibliographic information, author abstracts, and cited references found in 3,700 of the world's leading scholarly science and technical journals covering more than 100 disciplines. The Science Citation Index Expanded™ format, available through the Web of Science® and the online version, SciSearch®, cover more than 5,800 journals.

FEATURES -

1. Key Advantages & Capabilities
2. Allows researchers to conduct broad-based, comprehensive searches that uncover all the relevant information they need
3. Provides cited reference searching, the unique ISI search and retrieval feature that lets users track the literature forward, backward, and through the database, breaking through disciplinary and geographic boundaries
4. Enables users to conduct multidisciplinary searches to discover hidden subject relationships
5. Formats & Delivery Options
6. Internet and intranet — via Web of Science® - updated weekly; back-files to 1945
7. DVD (format available from late 2004 forward) — with author abstracts: updated monthly, includes annual cumulation on two discs; back-files to 1991.Without author abstracts: updated quarterly, includes annual cumulation on one disc; back-files to 1980; networking options
8. Online via distribution partners; updated weekly

SciSearch via DIALOG, DIMDI, and STN updated weekly; -1974, DataStar updated weekly; back-years to 1980 . Associated other products- Social Sciences Citation Index, Arts and Humanities Citation Index, Web of Science, Document Delivery and Information Management Tools.

35. What are different products of SCI?

A. Social Sciences Citation Index®—The Social Sciences Citation Index® (SSCI®) and Social SciSearch® provide access to current and retrospective bibliographic information, author abstracts, and cited references found in over 1,700 of the world's leading scholarly social sciences journals covering more than 50 disciplines. They also cover individually selected, relevant items from approximately 3,300 of the world's leading science and technology journals.

B. Arts and Humanities Citation Index®—The Arts & Humanities Citation Index® (A&HCI®) and Arts & Humanities Search® provide access to current and retrospective bibliographic information and cited references found in nearly 1,130 of the world's leading arts & humanities journals. They also cover individually selected, relevant items from approximately 7,000 of the world's leading science and social sciences journals.

C. Web of Science®—The Web of Science provides seamless access to current and retrospective multidisciplinary information from approximately 8,700 of the most prestigious, high impact research journals in the world. it also provides a unique search method, cited reference searching. With it, users can navigate forward, backward, and through the literature, searching all disciplines and time spans to uncover all the information relevant to their research. Users can also navigate to electronic full-text journal articles. Launched in January 2005, the Century of Science initiative makes hundreds of thousands of older, twentieth century scientific journal items available in one place and on one platform for the first time. Approximately 850,000 fully indexed journal articles have been added to Web of Science, from 262 scientific journals published in the first half of the twentieth century. This comprehensive collection is fully searchable, with complete bibliographic data, cited reference data and navigation, and direct links to the full text.

D. Document Delivery –

- Document Solution - Document Solution, a document delivery service, provides access to full-text items from virtually any publication within or outside of the ISI® database. This flexible, fast, and convenient service provides wide coverage, reliable customer support, fast and varied delivery options, and efficient management tools. (List of Electronically Stored Journals and Complete Journal List are given http://www.isinet.com/journals/).
- Thmson Patent Store - Obtain original patent documents

from around the world quickly and easily through the Thomson Patent Store, the new complete online source for patents. Via a single, user-friendly Web interface, you can directly view, download or request patents from anywhere in the world—no matter how difficult they are to locate. The Web-based document delivery service is automated, so turnaround and delivery are lightning quick—frequently taking just seconds! And it's highly cost-effective

E. Information Management Tools –

- ISI ResearchSoft — Bibliographic software solutions for managing references retrieved from ISI® or other online/ CD-ROM services
- EndNote®—The easy bibliography maker
- ProCite®—A flexible solution for managing references from the Internet to your bibliographies
- Reference Manager®—The powerful bibliographic desktop tool for workgroups, networks and collaborative projects
- RefViz®—A text analysis and visualization software program that provides users with an interactive display to explore references easily
- WriteNote®—A Web-based research and writing tool for students to organize references and write papers

F. Journal Citation Report—Provide Impact Factor (IF)/ Value of the journals covered in the SCI in each year with its IISN numbers etc.

4

Management of Libraries/Information Centres

36. Give importance of Scientific Management in the Libraries?

The term scientific management (SM) was first earned by Louis Brandies in 1910. It is concerned with the development of teamwork and a harmonies relationship between labour and management. It calls for establishing a correlation ship between rewords and efforts and for studying the reaction or response of workers to rest pauses and better working conditions. It is the application of science in management.

Principles of SM:

- Division of work
- Authority and responsibility should not be separated
- Unity of command
- Discipline/encompasses/accountability
- Subordination of individual interest to general interest
- Remuneration of staff/general salary structure
- Centralization of certain work and judicious distribution of work
- Chain of link
- Stability of tenure of staff and fairness & justice

Utility of SM in libraries:

- Provide scientific base for determining the salaries of the staff time to time
- Reorganize the staff for misuse of labour
- Increasing the efficiency and skillfulness of working staff members

Importance of SM in libraries:

- It helps in developing real facts and reasons of the libraries
- It helps in working efficiency of the staff in their routines
- It is the tool for personnel and financial management of the library.

37. How Decision can be taken, what are the Process of Decision-Making?

The decision-making is the heart of management. Manager of an organization performs all his tasks and functions through making decisions. He is continuously engaged in the decision making process while setting goals, determining plans and courses of action, formulating strategies, policies and procedures, assigning jobs to subordinates, guiding supervising and evaluating them.

Decisions are made through habitual as well as problem solving behaviour, when any problem come to a manager he thinks many options and choosing from among alternative courses of action. Thus it is the process of locating and defining the problem, developing alternative solutions to the problem, weighing the various alternative solutions in terms of their possible consequences, choosing the optimum solution from among them and implementing the decision effectively.

Decision making Process:

- Identification of the problem
- Analysis of the problem
- Development of alternative solutions
- Weighing alternative solutions
- Selection of the best alternative
- Implementation of the decision

Types of Decisions:

- Strategic- to achieve success for corporate goals in competition.
- Administrative- structuring of the organization
- Routine/tactical - routine decisions are unimportant need few alternatives for economic use.
- Programmed and non-programmed decisions
- Organizational and personal

38.Explain the Importance of Planning?

Planning is the most fundamental faction of management. It is deciding in advance the objectives of the organization and the means of attaining them. It is a kind of future picture and it entails the running of business as foreseen and providing against over a definite period. It is an analytical thought process, which covers:

- Assessment of the future
- Determination of objectives and goals in the light of the future
- Development of alternative courses of action to achieve such objective.
- Selection of the best course of action

Elements of Planning:

- What will be done
- What resources will be required?
- How it will be done
- Who will do it
- When it will be done

Importance in Libraries: A library can achieve following benefits from efficient planning:

- Concentrated on objectives
- Provides a sense of direction in the library
- Integrates diverse forces at work
- Reduces uncertainty
- Guides decision-making
- Provides a basis for orientation
- Improve competitive strength

39. Job Analysis: an Important Employment Tool how?

All hiring decisions and supervisory evaluations should be made on objective criteria. A supervisor needs to know each job under his or her supervision, and the qualifications needed to perform it, to develop objective interview questions and objectively evaluate an employees performance. Human resource specialists who are responsible for initial screening of job applicants and mediating performance appraisal disputes must also understand the key components of the jobs in their organization.

Job analysis provides an objective basis for hiring, evaluating, training, accommodating and supervising persons with disabilities, as well as improving the efficiency of your organization. It is a logical process to determine (1) purpose-the reason for the job, (2) essential functions-the job duties which are critical or fundamental to the performance of the job, (3) job setting-the work station and conditions where the essential functions are performed, and (4) job qualifications-the minimal skills an individual must possess to perform the essential functions. A job analysis describes the job, not the person who fills it.

How to Conduct a Job Analysis

The following questions can help you to analyze each job in your organization.

1. Purpose: What are the particular contributions of the job toward the accomplishment of the overall objective of the unit or organization?

2. Essential Functions:
   - What activities actually constitute the job? Is each really necessary
   - What is the relationship between each task
   - How many other employees are available to perform the job function? Can the performance of that job function be distributed among any other employees?
   - How much time is spent on the job performing each particular function?
   - What happens if a task is not completed on time?

3. Job Setting:
   - Location - Where are the essential functions of the job carried out?
   - Organization - How is the work organized for maximum safety and efficiency? How do workers obtain necessary equipment and materials?
   - Movement - What movement is required of employees to accomplish the essential functions of the job?
   - Conditions - What are the physical conditions of the job

4. Worker Qualifications:
   - What are the physical requirements (lifting, driving, cleaning, etc.)?
   - What are the general skills needed for the job (ability to read, write, add, etc.)?
   - What specific training is necessary? Can it be obtained on the job?
   - What previous experience, if any, can replace or be substituted for the specific training requirements?

How to Use the Job Analysis

Once the job analysis has been completed you will be in a better position to:

- Develop objective job-related interview questions.
- Write current and accurate position descriptions. Position descriptions should be updated on a regular basis and a job analysis done if any factors outlined above have to be altered.
- Perform objective performance appraisals.
- Determine if accommodations can assist a person with a disability to perform the job.
- Conduct personnel functions in a non-discriminatory manner.

40. Give Modern methods of budgeting in the libraries

Library budget is the central aspect of library finance, which serves as an instrument or control, communication, coordination, evaluation and motivation. It is the systematically prepared statement of estimated revenue and expenditure of the library for a period of time, usually a year. Budget is the guide to incur expenditure for different operations and activities of the library throughout he year. The general principle regarding the budget is that the income and expenditure of the library should balance each other.

There are different types of budgets: a) line item budgets (dived budget by items), b) program budgets (programmae/services), c) zero-based budgets (fresh budget every year), d) performance budgets (expenditure based on performance), Planning Programming budgeting System (PPBS) (it begins with goal/objectives and ends with programme/services) and five-year (or long-range) budget. An organization may choose to use any of these types of budgeting procedures.

In order to compile a budget, a manager needs to have a good understanding and knowledge of the library's expenses and sources of revenue and plans for future growth. Timelines are generally given in which current budget expenditures and revenues should be estimated. Future budgets are based upon costing forecasts derived from the current budget estimates. Managers need to be able to fully understand and produce a comprehensive budget as a plan for current, future and long-range library growth.

1. Budget History - examine budget statements and end-of-year statements for the last three years to get the history of the organization and determine trends. a) What are the expenses: Personnel, Postage, Collections development, Equipment, Maintenance etc, b) What are the sources of income.
2. Current budget
3. Budget Planning include-
   A. Prepare long-range financial plans, based on your library's mission statement and goals.
   B. Make recommendations to governing body for the next fiscal year.
   C. Formulate base budget to account for current levels of service for new fiscal year
   D. Add desired capital items to base budget

5

Information Technology

41. What is Virtual Library, what are its Evaluation Process?

Virtual Library (VL) is an organized set of links to items on the Internet network. The purpose of it is to enable users of a site to find relevant information, wherever it may reside on the network. or it is a system by which users access information that resides solely in electronic format on computer networks, without respect to physical location of the information. The virtual library exists independently of the amount or nature of the electronic information to which it provides access. There are no limits on the size, content or value of data in a virtual library. Its definition is shaped by individual or organizational need. A user in Washington, D.C., for example, can access, read, and print information from a computer located anywhere in the world.

VL Evolutionary Process

The virtual library did not arise out of the Internet—it's been evolving since the 1960s. During that period, both private and public libraries initiated innovative long-term projects to facilitate access to their continually expanding hard-copy collections. These programs integrated emerging information technologies with traditional printed materials. Libraries were among the first users of alternative media, such as microfiche and microfilm, tapes, sound recordings, and electronic files, which were the predecessors of today's online commercial database systems.

Early technology projects focused on the creation of electronic card catalogs known as OPACs (online public access catalogs). By the 1980s, the success of these ventures resulted in OPACs replacing traditional card catalogs in many academic, public, and special libraries. They also allowed libraries to engage in further cost-effective cooperative efforts to facilitate resource sharing and expand access to subject-specific resources beyond the walls of an individual library.

Another technology advancement involved the growth of electronic databases of subject-specific information such as ERIC (Educational Resources Information Center) and INSPEC (the Database for Physics, Electronics and Computing). These electronic databases quickly became an important information tools for libraries seeking to expand their resources beyond what they could physically house in their own collections.

But most of these databases were indexes only, leaving the users to locate copies of the actual text themselves. By the mid-1970s, full-text databases had been developed, and the legal community was quick to integrate them into their research operations. Today, proprietary full-text databases such as LEXIS and WESTLAW remain essentially unchallenged in the scope, depth, and quality of information that they provide to legal researchers. There are now creations of digital library all over world. There's no doubt that valuable information is available on the Internet through virtual library.

42. What is Information Technology

It includes all matters concerned with the furtherance of computer science and technology and with the design, development, installation, and implementation of information systems and applications [San Diego State University]. Information technology architecture is an integrated framework for acquiring and evolving IT to achieve strategic goals. It has both logical and technical components. Logical components include mission, functional and information requirements, system configurations, and information flows. Technical components include IT standards and rules that will be used to implement the logical architecture.

What are the Limitations of IT

- Job losses
- Faults in software (bugs or badly designed programs) can cause chaos.
- We are completely reliant on electricity
- GIGO (Data Validation can reduce the problem but not eliminate it)
- Information overload (e.g. people can be flooded with Email)
- Computer crime (hacking, viruses)

Remember: "To err is human but to really foul things up requires a computer". Great Computer Disasters of our time include: The London Ambulance Service, Substitution boards in USA World Cup, Y2K Bug (a warning that we are too reliant on computers?) and The I Love You virus.

43. What are the Benefits of ICT

From the Specification: "ICT systems offer fast repetitive processing, vast storage capability and the facility to search and combine data in many different ways that would otherwise be impossible."

- Increased speed of processing (e.g. MICR in a bank)
- Vast Storage capacity (compare filing cabinets to databases)
- Environmental gains (Can there be any such thing as the "paperless office"?)
- Read this article: The Paperless Office? Not by a long shot
- Ability to search and combine data in many different ways

(e.g. speed of searching a database vs. searching a filing cabinet)

- Instant Response (Real-time systems e.g. airline booking, credit card transactions. Compare with cheques which take three days to clear)
- Accurate Results (computers should be able to do a payroll for thousands of employees and not make a single mistake but only if they are well programmed)
- Communication (e.g. Email)
- Improved Company Image (better presentation of internal and external documents through use of DTP, Word Processing, Presentation Graphics BUT a lot of people with no sense of design make a mess when using WP and DTP)

44. What is Digital Library?

A digital library comprises digital collections, services and infrastructure to support lifelong learning, research, scholarly communication and preservation. A digital library is, like a traditional library, a collection of books and reference materials. Unlike a traditional library, however, the collection of a digital library is, as you would expect, digital, and is usually served over the World Wide Web. Some of the largest and most successful digital libraries are Project Gutenberg, bibliog. and the Internet Archive. Some people have criticized that copyright law hampers digital libraries, because works cannot be shared over different periods of time in the manner of a traditional library. The content is, in many cases, public domain or self-generated content only. Some digital libraries, such as Project Gutenberg, work to digitize out-of-copyright works and make them freely available to the public.

The Digital Library is:

- The collection of services
- And the collection of information objects
- That support users in dealing with information objects
- And the organization and presentation of those objects
- Available directly or indirectly
- Via electronic/digital means.

Advantages

- Universal access—people from all over the world could

gain access to the same information, as long as an Internet connection is available.

- Capacity—Whereas traditional libraries are limited by storage space, digital libraries have the potential to store much more information, simply because digital information require very little physical space to contain them.
- Cost—The cost of maintaining a digital library is much lower than that of a traditional library. A traditional library must spend large sums of money paying for staff, book maintance, rent, and additional books. Digital libraries do away with these fees.
- Any time, any day—Digital libraries can be accessed at any time of the day, where as traditional libraries have "operating hours".

Disadvantages

- Copyright—One difficulty to overcome for digital libraries is the way to distribute information. How does digital libraries distribute information at will while protecting the copyright of the author?
- Efficiency—With the much larger volume of digital information, finding the right material for a specific task become increasingly difficult.
- Environment—Digital libraries cannot reproduce the environment of a traditional library. Many people also find reading printed material to be easier than reading material on a computer screen.
- Preservation—Due to technological developments, a digital library can rapidly become out-of-date and its data may become inaccessible.

45. What are the Significance of CD ROM Technology

CD ROM stands for Compact Disc _ Read Only Memory, it permits the digital recording of information in the form of sound (audio), still images, video, text files and computer programmes on the same disc. Information is permanently written on the disc and cannot be modified. It is a plastic disc normally made out of poly carbonate, 4.72 inches in diameter, with a storage capacity of over 500 megabytes which is roughly equal to 250,000 pages of a text or 1500 floppy discs or 50 hard discs In 1980 Sony and Philips identified standards for Compact Disc Digital Audio (CD-A) and set in motion a technology that would revolutionize the delivery of entertainment and the storage of digital information. The initial use of the CD technology was linked to the production of music platters that operated through a sound system. In 1985 Sony and Philips introduced a standard for the storage of computer data—CD-ROM enabling the storage of vast amounts of data (654.74 MB) on a single CD disc. Since 1995 the developments in the technology have been ongoing and rapid and include: Compact Disc Interactive (CD-I), Compact Disc Television (CD-TV), Compact Disc Recording (CD-R) and Digital Video Disc (DVD). For most of the period the CD technology was used for entertainment and CD based video game systems and it was not until 1994 that CD-ROM players became a standard feature in personal computers.

Types of Compact Disc Format- There are four main types of Compact Disc format currently in use worldwide and they are:

- CD-A (Compact Disc Audio)
- CD-ROM (Compact Disc Read Only Memory)
- CD-I (Compact Disc Interactive)
- CD-ROM/XA (CD-ROM Extended Architecture).

The CD-ROM drives are classified by their rotational speed, which is based on the original speed of a CD-Audio. A double speed "2X" CD-ROM drive will run at twice the speed of a CD-Audio and an eight speed "8X" drive eight times faster. A quality hard disc in a computer currently transfers data at a rate of 3.8Mb/s. CD Speed Information transfer rate - 1X 150 Kb/s, 2X 300 Kb/s, 4X 600 Kb/s, 6X 900 Kb/s, 8X 1200 Kb/s, 12X 1800 Kb/s

In the case of video, large computer programmes and computer files the higher the transfer rate the smoother the operation and output. It is essential that the Central Processing Unit (CPU), hard disc drive and other computer components are enhanced to match the performance of the CD-ROM for optimum performance to be achieved.

The Current Status of Technology

Many factors have contributed to the popularity of CD-ROM and the main feature is the disc storage capacity of over 654.74MB or 74.5 minutes of audio. The cost of production and distribution compared with other methods of publishing is much lower. CD technologies allow for the simultaneous display of data in one or more forms including text, audio, video, still photographs and illustrations. The storage capacity of the disc freed users from inserting and removing numerous discs to access stored information or to run software programmes. Extensive resources, encyclopedias and databases became available on disc with the added advantage of search mechanisms that enabled information to be found and retrieved extremely quickly.

46. Importance of Users Education in Promoting Digital Information Services?

The rapid growth in information technology has changed the functioning of the libraries. The library is the nodal point of different network support service in the world now. Data base information system is developing and replace the traditional card catalogue system for identification and location of documents available in the library in this electronics era. So, the library is applying IT in its various services like:

- Internet/ E-email /Network/ database search services
- CD-ROM Search by subscribing CD-ROM databases and information package
- Resources sharing through local, regional, national and international networks
- CSA/SDI /Document Delivery/ collection etc.

Therefore, it is essential for every library to provide Users Education Programme(UEP) to know about the above services and its operation for providing the "right information to the right user at the right time" and this programme aims at educating the users to make use of the reading materials to greatest possible extent. Educating the users would introduce them to the right methods that would enable them to use libraries more effectively in research and development. The needs of such programmes are-

- To acquire the learning techniques
- To help in quick accessing and problem solving.
- To make users friendly use of the sophisticated equipment.
- To save the time of the users
- To maximum benefit of the library..

Levels of UEP:

- Library orientation and bibliographical instructions about the library to the user.

- Subject orientations are given to user more in-depth, explanation of specific library materials.
- Literature Search Training through internet/online/CD-ROM etc.

47. What is a Search Engine? How can we find our search results?

A search engine is the most common tool used to locate information on the Web. Google, Yahoo, AltaVista, AOLSearch, MSN, Excite, Lycos, Hotbot, Looksmart etc. are just examples of some general search engines that have been created to meet the demand for quickly finding information. Some important Indian Search Engines –

http://www.123india.com/

http://www.indiaconnect.com/

http://www.indiawebchakra.com/

http://www.newindia.com/seek/- Intelligent Indian Search Engine

http://www.samilan.com/- South Asian Milan

http://www.surfindia.com/

Search Queries—Search engines allow users to enter search terms known as keywords, which can be either words or phrases. The act of conducting a keyword search is called a search query. Example: Imagine you are looking for information on Albert Einstein. You can type his name into the search field of one of these engines. The search engine will scan a database for the keywords Albert Einstein and locate any Web pages that contain these words. Then the search engine will compile the relevant pages and generate a list of their URLs.

Search Results—It's important to know that not all search engines deliver the same results. First of all, different engines search different databases for the information you specify in your search query. Some databases are more sophisticated and more detailed than others. Secondly, the organization of search results varies, depending on the search engine you are using. Generally, the results at the top of the page are what the search engine interprets as the most relevant to your search. However, not all search engines measure relevancy in the same way. For example, with many search engines, a Web page will have a higher ranking in the list of results if your keywords appear many times throughout the Web page—in the title, near the beginning, or close together on the page. For these reasons, you should never rely on just one search engine when you're conducting research on the Web. Try using more than one engine; doing so will likely yield better, richer results!

48. What is a Meta-search Engine?

A meta-search engine scans multiple search engines simultaneously and provides results based on the keyword(s) submitted. Meta-search engines can save time, but it's best not to rely on them exclusively. Since search engines interpret search terms differently, one or more of them might misunderstand your keyword(s). Before using a meta-search engine, find out how it compiles results. This information usually appears on a site's Help page. Some of the important Meta search engines are Dogpile, Vivisimo, Kartro, Mamma, SurfWax etc.

How Do They Work?- In a meta-search engine, you submit keywords in its search box, and it transmits your search simultaneously to several individual search engines and their databases of web pages. Within a few seconds, you get back results from all the search engines queried. Meta-search engines do not own a database of Web pages; they send your search terms to the databases maintained by search engine companies. Vivísimo is a meta-search engine that allows users to search the Web or specific sites such as MSN™ and Lycos ®. Be aware that Vivísimo only searches URLs, titles, and descriptions from other search engines' results pages and not the actual Web sites themselves. Vivísimo also features a new technology called a clustering engine, which organizes search results into categories.

49. What is a Directory?

A directory, also known as a subject directory, refers to any collection of Web sites organized into such categories as health, history, sports, arts and entertainment, and travel. (Each directory has its own unique categories and links.) Search engines, including Yahoo! and Google, include directories as one search option. Library Web sites also typically have directory listings.

How Does a Directory Work?

Most directories have a hierarchical organization, meaning that the categories are initially arranged by general topics, which then become more specific as you "drill down" into the various subcategories. Example: If you are using a directory and looking for information on the Cold War, you might first look at how that directory groups its Web sites. Chances are, you'd want to look for a History subcategory. Within History, you might find such groupings as U.S. History, World History, and Ancient World History. You'd continue down this path until you found Web sites that focus on the Cold War.

50. What are the Key Differences Between Search Engines and Directories?

Search engines recognize the keywords you submit and will list hundreds of thousands of unordered results. Unfortunately, as good and quick as the search engine technology is, it can't recommend which sites to visit and which to avoid. A search engine does not discriminate. A directory, however, does. A directory is someone's attempt to find the best sites on the Web for a range of given topics. The person, business, organization, or institution responsible for creating that directory has already weeded out the bad sites and found the most useful. A directory can be a great place to start your research. In a relatively short amount of time, you can get a good sense of what's available on your research topic.

51. What is Cyber Crime?

There is no single definition of cyber crime. Cyber crimes are unlawful activities in cyberspace brought about by computer experts and they constitute of hackers, crackers, disgruntled employees and even by children. Cyber crimes can be generated from digital library, cyber café, computer lab and office or even from home PC where Internet connections are available. Cyber crime can be brought about against person, property and government.

52. Why Cyber Crimes?

Cyber crimes are happening everywhere now throughout the world.

- Web jacking–jacking of particular website for specific interest. Example hacking of Ministry of IT Govt. of India website.

- Virus attack–Onel DeGurman of Philippines floated "I LOVE YOU" virus on the net in the year 2000. The boy was escaped due to no Cyber Low at that time.
- Hacking–two Indian computer trainers were arrested in January 2001 for allegedly trying to hack into the computers of State Bank of India.
- Denial of Service Attack–The Internet Service Provider (ISP) was badly hit in January 2001: consequently computers were unable to exchange messages for a period of about a week.

Computer crimes have tremendous potential to hit mankind with unbelievable severity. Consciousness about such threat is to be increased among the stakeholders and adequate attempts have to be taken to counter it, otherwise it will surely eat into the vitals of our nation as well as world beauty. Key factors contributing the growth of cyber crimes in Indian scenario are as follows- lack of awareness; law-enforcing agencies are not yet to be furnished with expert manpower and cyber forensic tools. Cyber victims are not lodge any complain due to fear and loss of public confidence. The cyber criminals should not equip with sophisticated technology and punished by low.

53. Types of Cyber Crimes

There are different ways through which cyber criminals are committing cyber crimes round the globe. Some are as follows-

- *Cyber defamation:* This is an attempt to defame a person or an organization using virtual medium email.
- *Cyber plagiarism:* This is the use of words and ideas of an author, obtained through electronic media without acknowledgement.
- *Cyber pornography:* It is stimulating sexual or other erotic activities via the Internet.
- *Denial of service attack:* It is an incident in which networked computers are disconnecting from network by corrupt programmes
- *Email bombing:* It is sending excessive amount of email to an individual or company or even mail servers repeatedly.
- *Hacking:* It is an unauthorized access to computer systems or network or databases.

- *Web jacking*: It is controlling of websites by another. The hacker may distort the information of the target website.
- *Steganography*: It is a technique of transmitting hidden message through computer.

54. How to Save the Library from Cyber Crimes?

Digital libraries or automated libraries are also becoming the victims of cyber crimes. So these libraries have following protection to prevent for save working.

- System Protection- Latest ant virus software is to be installed and should be updated time to time. Hard disk should be scanned frequently to detect virus. Firewalls should be used to keep private networks secure from Internet attack. Like Firewall, Intrusion Detection System (IDS) can also protect a computer against internal attacks.
- Encryption- It is a technique to hide computer related information from others for the purpose of security. This can be adapted in the libraries.
- Email Attachment Strangers – stranger are floating viruses for every email attachment should be strictly avoided.
- User Identification and authentification- Proper password protection should be used.
- Procurement/Downloading/Recording- Software should be procured from reliable sources, free software or down loading from Internet etc be avoided.
- Use of Preventive Software for Misuse of Net- Chatting, playing games, sending useless E-mail, downloading of textual matters or pictures or free software etc. are the common misuses of Internet. These will lead to virus contamination, memory jam and wastage of useful bandwidth. Some Software relating to prevention of misuse of unethical and illegal activities with computers exists through out the globe are – KidWatch Time Control, SpamBouncer, Track4Win, Surfwall, Net Nanny, Cyber Sentinel and Crime Soft etc. Therefore several private sector organizations like Tata Consultancy Services, Birlasoft, Hero Honda, Plaries, BPL, ICICI etc have taken measures to deal with unscrupulous activities. It is right time for modern libraries to take adequate measures to pave their way to the world of frictionless journey.

55. What are Cyber Laws?

Cyber Low deals with legal issues of cyberspace, due to offensive activities are increasing in Internet. Hence, Lows must be formulated to monitor these activates. Some countries have been rather vigilant and formed some lows to protect cyber crimes. The Government of India has also enacted "The Information Technology Act" in 2000 to tackle computer related crime. International Initiative are also continuing for this lows. G-8 (USA, UK, USSA, France, Germany, Canada, and Japan & Italy), The Council of Europe (COE) and SAARC (South Asian Association for Regional Cooperation) countries (India, Pakistan, SriLanka, Maldives, Bangladesh, and Bhutan & Nepal) have discussed to enact Cyber Lows to prevent Cyber Crime. In our country the IT Act-2000 is working since June 19 2000, which has 13 chapters and 93 sections along with 4 schedules. Chapter IX and XI deals with various cyber crimes and it prescribe specific punishment for different kinds of offences. A few relevant sections are given below:-

- Damaging Computer, computer System etc. (IT Act, Sec-43)—States that unauthorized access, denial of access to information to authorized user, damaging with virus or tampering or manipulating any computer/system/network are serious crimes. Any miscreant committed is liable to pay compensation not exceeding 1 crore rupees to victim.
- Tempering with Computer Sources Documents (IT Act, Sec-65)—Whoever knowingly or intentionally any individual organisation causes another to conceals, destroys, alter any computer sources/code/data etc. shall be punishable with 3 year imprisonment or fine upto 2 lakh or with both.
- Hacking with Computer system (IT Act, Sec-66)—Whoever likely to cause wrongful loss or damage to the public or any person destroys or delets or alter any information of a computer or hack shall be punished with imprisonment up to 3 years or fine upto 3 lakh or both.
- Obscene Electronics Publication (IT Act, Sec-67)—Whoever publishes or transmits or causes to be published in the electronic form. ...Shall be punished on first conviction with imprisonment for 5 years with 1 lakh fine.

- Protected System (IT Act, Sec-70)—Whomever access to protected system of any computer shall be imprison for 10 years and shall also be liable to fine.

Implementation/Amendment of Cyber Low

The It Act 2000 along with other Indian acts can implement a good framework to fight against cyber crimes in Indian soil. Dr. Monmohan Singh (P.M. of India) is now emphasizing to tighten laws to protect the country against cyber crimes. India has established some of its police stations to handle cyber crimes at .Bangalore-560001, Chennai – 600008, Hederabad – 500004 and Mumbai. The first cyber crime police station was started at Bangalore. The CBI has set up Cyber Investigation Cell and Cyber Crime Research & Development Unit to collect information regarding cyber crimes occurring through out the country.

With the advancement of Internet or e-technology and due to some loopholes in the IT Act, there are also some difficulties to capture/ punish the cyber crime hence the Act should be timely amended time to time. The following acts of the country have been amended in order to keep parity with the Information Technology Act 2000: Indian Penal Code-1860, Indian Evidence Act-1872, Indian Telegraph Act –1885, Banker's Book Evidence Act–1891 and Reserve Bank of India Act–1934.. There are some trends in India for which some of the educational courses are incorporating cyber lows in relevant curriculum.

MULTIPLE CHOICE QUESTION/ANSWER

A: Information & Communication

1. The Term information science come into existence in;
   a. 1960 b. 1959
   c. 1958 d. 1961
2. Transborder data flow refers to:
   a. Exchange of document between boundaries/countries
   b. Free flow of books between countries
   c. Exchange of electronics information between countries
   d. Free flow of data between countries
3. "Half life" of Information implies that:
   a. Information is useful only half the time
   b. As information ages it is used less
   c. The life of the information is reduced

d. Dead information is not used

4. Which is the following is in the correct sequence

a. Data -	Knowledge-	Information-	Wisdom-
b. Data-	Information-	Knowledge-	Wisdom
c. Information-	Data-	Wisdom-	Knowledge
d. Information-	Knowledge-	Knowledge-	Wisdom

5. Topmost consumer of Information are:

a. Data -	Knowledge-	Information-	Wisdom-
a. Teacher	b. Information Personnel	c. Researcher and Scientist	
d. Students			

6. The draft policy document on Library & Information System in India is submitted in:

a. May 1986	b. June 1987	c. April 1988	d. October 1985

7. NISSAT is established in the year:

a. 1972	b. 1971	c. 1970	d. 1977

8. CODATA stand for:

a. Commission on Data for Technology

b. Committee on Data for Science & Technology

c. Committee on Development for Science and Technology

d. Commission on Development for Science and Technology

9. The correct sequence of information flow is :

a. Message -	Source-	Channel -	Receiver
b. Message -	Source-	Medium-	Receiver
c. Source-	Message -	Channel -	Receiver
d. Source-	Channel -	Message -	Receiver

10. Intellectual Property Right are recognized by:

a. Copyright Low	b. Patent Low	c. Both a & b	d. Nither a & b

11. The Book "Communication " is written by :

a. ZE D Johnson	b. Alisen Kent	c. E Rawley	d. D A Kemp

12. "Documentation and Information" is written by:

a. S R Ranganathan	b. A K Mukharji	c. J H Shera	d. B Gura

13. "Towords Paperless Information System" is written by:

e. F W Lancaster	f. Andre Shaw	g. James Cameron	h. J H Shera

14. The"Mathematical Theory of Communication" was first developed by:

a. Clando Shanon	b. Lasswell	c. Khittermore	d. Allen Kent

15. Copy right Bulletin is Published by:

a. Aslib	b. UNESCO	c. LA	d. ALA

16. The Indian library Association was founded at...
a. Madras in 1945 b. Delhi in 1950 c. Calcutta in 1933 d. Bombay in 1927

17. The first librarian of National Library, Calcutta was....
a. G Bhattacharya b. B Guha c. B S Keshvan d. K P Sinha

18. What was the name of the National Library of India before independence:
a. Asiatic Society Library, Bengal b. British Council Library
c. Imperial Library d. Calcutta Public Libraryu

19. The National Science Library is a part of ....
a. INSDOC b. UGC c. NISCAIR d. NISSAT

20. National Union Catalogue of Scientific Serials in India (NUCSSI) is published by....
a. INSDOC b. SENDOC c. INIS d. NASSDOC

B: Information and Reference Sources/Services

21. Who published the Indian National Bibliography (INB):
a. Delhi Public Library b. Central Reference Library, Madrasc Central Reference Library, Calcutta d. NISSAT

22. Social Science, Science Citation Index is published by:
a. NISSAT, New Delhi b. RR Bowker
c. INSDOC d. Institute for Scientific Information (ISI), Philadelphia

23. "Indian Books in Print" is an example of
a. Local Bibliography b. National Bibliography
c. Trade Bibliography d. Analytical Bibliography

24. "World of Learning" is a:
a. Annual Bibliography b. Dictionary
c. Directory d. Bibliography

25. The first Encyclopaedia "Historia Naturalis" was published in the
a. 77 AD b. 1024 AD c. 1810 AD d. 1425 AD

26. "Ulrich International Periodical Directory" is a which kind of source of information:
a. Tertiary b. Secondary c. Reference d. Primary

27. ERIC database sponsored by the Department of Health Education & Welfare, Govt of USA, deals:
a. Economics b. Energy c. Ethics d. Education

28. "british National Bibliography" is published:
a. Yearly b. Bimonthly c. Weekly d. Daily

29. New York Times Index, Indian Press Index and News Paper Index are example of Indexing Service devoted to :

a. Journal b. Periodicals c. Newspaper d. Report Literature

30. Which kind of bibliography is a systematic list of all the books published all over the world:

a. Author b. Universal c. Trade d. Title

C: Information Processing & Organisation/Retrieval

31. The second largest Journal publisher in the world by number of journals published

a. John Wiley b. Springer c. Read Elsevier d. Blackwell

32. Which form of filing is also called "Nothing before Something" method:
   a. Word-by-Word arrangement
   b. Letter by Letter
   c. Dictionary
   d. Alphabetical
33. What is standard size of a catalogue card:
   a. 14cmX7cm
   b. 12.5X7.5cm
   c. 10.5cmX5.5cm
   d. 12.7cmX7.6cm
34. Match the following cataloguing codes with the years given below:

a. AACRI b. AACR-II

c. ALA Code d. CCC

i. 1978 ii. 1967

iii. 1934 iv. 1949

- a-I,b-ii,c-iii,d-iv
- a-I,b-ii,c-iii,d-iv
- a-I,b-ii,c-iii,d-iv
- a-ii,b-I,c-iv,d-iii

35. Cataloguing is a process and catalogue is a ......

a. Service b. Machine c. Stationary d. Tool

36. The area of the Main Entry where the name of a person, a corporate body, pseudonym or the title of the book is written is known as:
   a. Coll No. section
   b. Descriptive element area
   c. Heading area
   d. Collation area
37. Data comprising author, publisher, title, place and year

of publication, number of pages and illustration etc. is called:

a. Annotation
b. Imprint
c. Standard format
d. Bibliographical data

38. Machine Readable catalogue (MARC) finally come into existence in :

a. 1966 b. 1968 c. 1956 d. 1969

39. According to AACR-II, in case of a publication by the Lok Sabha, the entry would be made under:

a. India, LokSabha
b. India, Parliament, Lok Sabha
c. India.Parliament. Lok Sabha
d. Lok Sabha(India)

40. In CCC, the Class Index Entry is derived from the:

a. Book Number
b. Class Number
c. Call Number
d. Accession Number

41. According to CCC, if articles by different authors are published under one title, it is known as

a. Composite Book
b. Artificial Composite Book
c. Festschrift
d. Ordinary Composite Book

42. The MARC 21 tag that maps to Dublin Core's coverage is

a. 100 and 110
b. 720 and 740
c. 651, 752
d. 506, 540

43. Ranganathan has postulated five fundamental categories as:

a. Part, Process, Place, Time, action
b. Personality, Matter, energy, Space, Time
c. Product, Matter, Energy, space, Time
d. None of the Above

44. There are two kinds of tables in UDC namely:

a. Main & Auxiliary

b. ACI & PCI
c. Form Division & SS Division
d. General & Special

45. In which scheme of classification zero (0) is used for time isolates
a. CC
b. UDC
c. DDC
d. None of the Above

46. In DDC special topic are introduced the standard subdivision number-
a. 07 b. 03 c. 04 d. 05

47. In MARC 21, the security classification is introduced by the field
a. Author b. Universal c. Trade d. Title
a. 520 b. 355 c. 365 d. 535

48. The concept of literary warrant was introduced by-
a. Sayers b. Ranganathan c. Hulme d. Brown

49. Blob world is
a. A Portal of Blog aficionados
b. A method of Blogging
c. A CBIVR based retrieval tool
d. None of the above

50. The International Children library is developed at
a. University of California, Berkeley
b. University of Texas at Austin
c. University of Maryland
d. University of Illinois, Urbana Champaign

D: Management of Libraries/Inf. Centre

51. The Internet Public Library uses the following retrieval method
a. Relevance ranking method
b. Uses the Boolean matching
c. The Hot Link method
d. The Probablistic method

52. If things can go wrong, it will is called the
a. Murphy law
b. Kelly law
c. Metcalf law

d. Bush law

53. Critical Path Method (CPM) and Programme Evaluation & Review Technology(PERT) are used for improving the quality of:
   a. Budgeting
   b. Reporting
   c. Modern
   d. None of these

54. The assessment of the right type of staff to be entrusted with the various activities calls for the use of management technique known as :
   a. Job description
   b. Job assessment
   c. Job analysis
   d. Staff analysis

55. Library cess is one of the sources of finance for which kind of libraries
   a. Public
   b. Academic
   c. Special
   d. Business

56. POSDCoRB Iis given by:
   a. Luther Gullick & Lyndall Urwick
   b. FW Taylor & Gullick
   c. L Gullick & Wilson Kiplector
   d. F Talor & M Johson

57. "Managerial Grid" is also colled as:
   a. Primary Grid
   b. Authority Grid
   c. Leadership Grid
   d. Classical Grid

58. The concept of "Quality Circle" was developed in:

a. Japan b. USA c. UK d. India

59. Path Goal Thery of Leadership is developed by:

a. Robert House b. R Likert c. J Thomson d. H Fayol

60. Delphy method is used for:

a. Planning b. Budgeting c. Forcasting d. Evaluation

E: Information Technology

61. Wiki is

a. Means quick b. A Software c. Both a & b d. Neither of the two

62. Soople is
 a. Google simple Advanced search
 b. Google expert search
 c. Google easy expert search
 d. Simple Object Oriented Public Key Language
63. IBID (India Business Insight Database) is accessible to global users through
 a. Fictive b. Dialog c. Both a&b d. None
64. The Scientists of the world who are ranked among the top 1 percent of highly cited scientists are listed at
 a. www.wos.com
 b. isihighlycited.com
 c. highlycitedauthors.com
 d. citationindex.com
65. Mark the - Odd one out - from the following:
 a. Knovel b. NetLibrary c. Ebrary d. Cybrary
66. Choose the odd one
 a. Compendex b. MicroPatent c. Deplhion d. IEL database
67. The premier institution for Standardization of different operation in a library in India is
 a. Bureau of Indian Standards
 b. Institute of Indian Standards
 c. Indian Standards Centre
 d. Indian Standards Bureau
68. National Library for the Blind is situated at:
 a. Ahmedabad b. Bombay c. Calcutta d. Dehradun
69. Science and Technology Policies Information Exchange System (SPINES) programme was promoted by
 a. UNESCO b. ILO c. UNIDO d. IAEA
70. IP address to host name translation is handled by
 a. DNS
 b. TCP/IP protocol
 c. IP-Hostname translator
 d. None of these
71. Hyper Card was developed by
 a. V. Bush b. Engelbart c. Ted Nelson d. B. Atkinson
72. The institution which is not participating for LOCKSS (Lots of Copies Keep Stuff Safe) programme in India is

a. Indian Institute of Management, Kozhikode
b. Tata Institute of Fundamental Research, Mumbai
c. JRD Tata Memorial Library, IISc, Bangalore
d. Jawaharlal Nehru University (JNU), Delhi

73. The display of an XML document is achieved by
a. The Browser alone
b. The Browser and the DTD
c. The Browser and the XSL
d. None of the above

74. Each year National Library Day is observed on:
a. 19 November b. 15 August c. 12 August d. 14 November

75. Zipf law relates to:
a. Productivity of an author
b. Productivity of an periodical title
c. Frequency of word occurrences in a text
d. Frequency of use of a periodical in a library

76. Who is regarded as the first classificationist to make an attempt to formulate a theory for Library Classification?
a. W.C.B. Sayers
b. S R Ranganathan
c. H.E. Bliss
d. Melvil Dewey

77. The term Informatics was proposed by :
a. Garfield
b. Mikhailov
c. Borko
d. Ranganathan

78. The term cyber means and was coined by
a. Behind and coined by William Gibson
b. Control and was coined by William Gibson
c. Governor and was coined by Norbert Wiener

79. Page jacking is a technique of
a. Stealing information from a website
b. Is a technique of redirecting traffic to another website
c. Is submitting stolen information to a search engine
d. All of them

80. The number of encoding forms that UNICODE standard defines are
a. Four b. Two c. Three d. Five

81. Alexandria Digital Library is

a. One of the six DL projects in the DLI 1
b. Spatial data digital library
c. Based at the University of California, Santa Barbara
d. All of the above

82. E-Journal Portal that indexes articles from the largest number of Open Access Journals in the World

a. DOAJ b. Ingenta c. Oaister d. J-Gate

83. UMI is the
a. Brand name of microfilm products by the Company Proquest Inc.
b. Is the old name of the Company ProQuest Inc.
c. Is the microfilm archive Theses and Dissertation
d. A name that no longer exists

84. Open Access Initiative (OAI) has evolved into two models. One of them, Author pays model is called Gold Route. The other one is Author pays model. What is it called?
a. Red Route
b. Green Route
c. Platinum Route
d. Silver Route

85. The man one who developed the TCP/IP protocol is
a. Tim Berners Lee
b. Vinton G Cerf
c. Brewster Kahle
d. None of the above

86. 404 Not Found is an error message that appears
a. When URL or the link is wrong
b. When it has been changed
c. Either of the two
d. Both

87. Gathering schedule refers to
a. The Time line followed by libraries for e-Journals
b. The schedule for taking a snap shot of the websites for Web Archiving
c. The Time Line for crawlers
d. None of the above

88. The Classification Scheme that is based on the facet analysis of Ranganathan
a. Brown Subject Classification
b. Bliss Bibliographic Classification

c. Both
d. None of the above

89. The concept of 'Relative Location was introduced by-
a. Ranganathan b. Dewey c. Brown d. Bliss

90. The CERN Document Server
a. Is a software for managing book collections
b. Is a Web Server Software
c. Is Open Source digital library software
d. Is a software for managing internal documents

91. One the most important digital libraries in the humanities is-
a. Melville
b. California Digital Library
c. Perseus
d. Gutenberg

92. EnCompas from Endeavour uses the following for link resolving
a. LinkFinderPlus b. SFX c. Hyperion d. Igate

93. Cross Language Information Retrieval is accomplished by
a. Machine Translation
b. Multilingual Thesauri
c. Language Independent Metadata
d. Any one of the above

94. Wikipedia was developed by
a. Jimmy Wales
b. Walter Scott
c. Linus Torvalds
d. None of the above

95. South Asian Literary Recording Project
a. Is a Project of CSAL
b. Is a Project of LOC, New Delhi
c. Is a Project of University of Chicago
d. Is project of the University of Maryland

96. PEAK is a collaborative Project on
a. Pricing of access to e-Journals
b. People Access to Knowledge
c. Performing and Entertaining Artists Knowledge portal
d. None of the above

97. DigiCult is a Programme of the

a. Information Society Technologies
b. DLF
c. Educause
d. CNI

98. The Dublin Core element Source covers
a. The type of software required to open the digital object
b. The Source code of the digital object
c. Information about the DOI
d. None of the above

99. MPEG 21 is
a. Is standard for multimedia content across devices
b. Is a metadata standard for multimedia metadata
c. Neither
d. Both a & b

100. The PageRank is named after
a. The Algorithm used
b. An Eponymous term
c. A search engine
d. The rule based technique

Answers of Multiple Choice Questions (1-100)

1.b	11.a	21.c	31.b	41.d	51.a	61.c	71.d	81.d	91.c
2.c	12.d	22.d	32.a	42.c	52.a	62.c	72.d	82.d	92.a
3.b	13.e	23.c	33.b	43.b	53.d	63.c	73.c	83.a	93.d
4.b	14.a	24.c	34.a	44.a	54.c	64.b	74.d	84.b	94.a
5.c	15.b	25.a	35.d	45.c	55.a	65.d	75.c	85.b	95.b
6.a	16.c	26.b	36.b	46.c	56.a	66.d	76.a	86.c	96.a
7.d	17.c	27.d	37.d	47.b	57.c	67.d	77.b	87.c	97.a
8.b	18.c	28.b	38.a	48.c	58.a	68.d	78.c	88.b	98.d
9.c	19.c	29.c	39.c	49.c	59.a	69.a	79.d	89.b	99.d
10.c	20.a	30.b	40.b	50.c	60.c	70.a	80.c	90.c	100.b

SECTION III

SHORT/OBJECTIVE TYPE FOR BOTH INTERVIEW/ WRITTEN

1

Contribution of Prof. S.R. Ranganathar

His Life in Short

Shiyali Ramamrita Ranganathan (*Born:* Aug. 9, 1892 at Shiyali, Madras, India. *Died:* Sept. 27, 1972 at Bangalore, Mysore) was an innovative mathematician and librarian from India. His most notable contributions to the field were his five laws of library science and the development of the first major analytico-synthetic classification system, the Colon classification. He is considered to be the father of library science in India.

- ❑ He was educated at the Hindu High School in Shiyali, at Madras Christian College (where he took B.A. and M.A. degrees in mathematics in 1913 and 1916), and at Teachers College, Saidapet.
- ❑ In 1917 he joined the faculty of Government College, Mangalore.
- ❑ From 1920 to 1923 he subsequently taught at Government College, Coimbatore, and at Presidency College, University of Madras, in 1921-1923.
- ❑ In 1924 he was appointed first librarian of the University of Madras, and in order to fit himself for the post he traveled to England to study at University College, London.
- ❑ From 1925 to 1944 he took up the job at Madras in earnest in 1925 and held it until 1944.
- ❑ Elected as President of ILA at Jaipur Conference in 1944-1953. D> Lit by Delhi Univ.in 1948.
- ❑ From 1945 to 1954 he served as librarian and as professor of library Science at Hindu University in Varanasi

(Banaras), and from 1947 to 1954 he taught at the University of Delhi.

- Worked as Editor -Annal of Lib. Science (1956-1963), ABGILA and Lib. Sc with Slant to Doc.
- From 1954 to 1957 he was engaged in research and writing in Zurich.
- Awarded Padamashree in 1957
- He returned to India in the latter year and served as visiting professor at Vikram University, Ujjain, until 1959.
- In 1962 he founded and became head of the Documentation Research and Training Centre in Bangalore, with which he remained associated for the rest of his life, and in 1965 he was honoured by the Indian government with the title of national research professor in library science.

His Contribution to Library Science

1. *Five Laws of Library Science*—The most far-reaching effect of Ranganathan's contribution flows from his formulation of the Five Laws of Library Science.
   - Books are for use
   - Every reader his/her book
   - Every book, its reader
   - Save the time of the reader
   - A library is a growing organism

B.I Palmer said that the laws were "succinct statements of reasons of our profession". Ranganathan himself described the impact of the Five laws on his later works. He said: "The integral quality of the entire domain, with the focus on the Five Laws at the Zenith of the Spiral of Scientific Method, is well reflected in the family of about four dozen books of mine. The ancestor of this family is the Five Laws of Library Science (1931). All the books form a single unit. Indeed, they are like chapters of one huge book".

2. Classification—Ranganathan felt dissatisfied at the inability of the Decimal Classification, then widely prevalent, to accomodate the newly emerging subjects . He thus emerged a new species of classification: Analytico-Synthetic Classification". The Colon Classification, published in 1933, was the result of this triggering experience. The system assumed that each subject in the universe of subjects can be analysed into facets. In due

course came the concepts of basic facet, isolate facet, and spectators. These isolate facets were later postulated to be the manifestation of one or another - and of one and only one - of the Five Fundamental Categories: Personality, Matter, Energy, Space, Time. After a deep and incessant struggle, his magnum opus in classification, the Prolegomena to Library Classification, was published in 1937. This gave, for the first time, an integrated set of canons and principles to guide the design of a scheme for classification and for the classification of subjects according to a scheme.

3. Cataloguing—The first major contribution of Ranganathan to cataloguing was the design of the Classified Catalogue Code, published in 1935. It was probably the first comprehensive code for a classified catalog. After the publication of the CCC, Ranganathan turned his attention toward developing a theory of cataloguing. Between 1934 and 1937, some of the rules of CCC from time to time cape up for critical examination. On the anvil of such critical discussions, certain normative principles of cataloguing took shape. Though these were the implications of the Five Laws, they formed a distinct set of normative principles governing cataloguing theory and practice. These were the canons of cataloguing. The experience was recorded in the Theory of Library Catalogue. This book gave, for the first time, a comprehensive and dynamic theory of cataloguing.
4. Chain Procedure—The Chain Procedure for deriving subject index entries is a very widely accepted contribution of Ranganathan. It was experimented within the Madras University Library. It gave a facile method for deriving the headings for subject index entries. In 1950, it was applied on a large scale in the production of the British National Bibliography.
5. Book Selection—Ranganathan's contribution to the theory of book selection was principally derived from the Five Laws of Library Science.
6. Library Administration and Management—Ranganthan started the rationalization of library routines in 1925 when he took full charge of the administration of the Madras University Library. He estimated that library work can be broken down into one-thousand-odd jobs.

Ranganathan's theory of library management isolates the following distinctive factors of work: Planning, Job analysis, Routine, Elimination of waste, Correlation, Time Scheme, Forms and registers, Correspondence files and records

7. Organisation and Library Systems—He aimed at developing a legislation-based library network for pulbic libraries.
8. Library Housing—Ranganathan crystallized the theory and practice for library buildings and furntiture through a pragmatic analysis of the functional layout needed for a library building.

2

Library Legislation in India

On a look at the existing library scenario prevailing in the country, it appears that there are several public library systems, as stated below: The British Government in India entrusted public library services to the local bodies (Municipalities in the urban areas and District Boards in the rural areas) in keeping with the practice in their own country. However, the local bodies were not empowered to levy library cess to finance public library services. Thus, the expenditure on public library had to be met from the consolidated fund of the local body concerned. If we go back to trace the genesis of public library system in the country, it is observed that as back as in 1957, the Sinha Committee was appointed by the Govt. of India to review the public library system and suggest measures for its future development. On the recommendation of the Sinha Committee, the Sen Committee was appointed in 1963 and recommended, for better public library services in the courtry and the hierarchical structure of public libraries, based largely on Madras Public Library Services Act,

1948. It is observed that out of 29 States and 6 Union Territory Administrations, only 12 states have so far passed library legislation in India.

1. Tamilnadu Public Libraries Act, 1948 having provision for library cess (10%) on property tax;
2. Andhra Pradesh Public Libraries Act, 1960 having provision for library cess (8%) on lands and buildings;
3. Karnataka Public Libraries Act, 1965 having provision for library cess (6%) on lands, buildings, vehicles and profession;
4. Maharashtra Public Libraries Act, 1967 - No library cess - State Government meets the expenditure;
5. West Bengal Public Libraries Act, 1979 - No library cess - State Government meets the expenditure;
6. Manipur Public Libraries Act, 1988-No library cess;
7. Kerala Public Libraries Act, 1989 having provision for library cess (5%) on property tax and not less than 1% of State expenditure on education;
8. Haryana Public Libraries Act, 1989 - Local bodies to levy cess;
9. Goa Public Libraries Act, 1993 - Surcharge on IFML @ 0.50 ps. Per ltr. And 0.50 ps. On bulk bear per ltr. And 1% on State Education Budget;
10. Mizoram Public Libraries Act, 1983 - No library cess-State Govt. meets the expenditure;
11. Gujarat Public Libraries Act, 2002 - No library cess
12. Orissa Public Libraries Act, 2002 - No library cess.

3

Important Library (Resources) Journals

List of Some International LIS Journals

1. ALA TechSource—Home of Library Technology Reports Online, how-to guides to library systems and services, plus the Source Online, a site with free news, features, and

commentary.

2. American Libraries Online—Online version of the American Library Association's flagship publication. Features current news about libraries and librarians. Includes job opportunities.
3. Annual Review of Information Science and Technology—Focuses on activities and trends in the field of information science and technology. Includes links to the ASIS home page and print version purchase information.
4. Cataloging & Classification Quarterly—Editorial information, tables of contents and abstracts.
5. College and Research Libraries—Flagship peer-reviewed publication of the Association of College and Research Libraries (ACRL). Links to table of contents and book reviews from 1997 to the present.
6. Computers in Libraries—Online version of the monthly magazine focusing on library oriented information technology.
7. Cybermetrics. Electronic journal of scientometrics, informetrics and bibliometrics—An electronic journal devoted to the description and analysis of the Internet as scholarly communication tool.
8. D-Lib Magazine—Monthly publication about research and innovation in digital libraries.
9. E-JASL: The Electronic Journal of Academic and Special Librarianship—Independent, professional, refereed journal dedicated to advancing knowledge and research in the areas of academic and special librarianship.
10. E-LIS—Open access archive of preprints, postprints and other documents in the field of library and information science.
11.) Future of Print Media Journal—A quarterly online journal about the digital transformation of printing and publishing.
12. IFLA Journal—Journal of the International Federation of Library Associations and Institutions, an international organization focusing on libraries and library users. Contains tables of contents, abstracts and some full text beginning with 1993.
13. Information Processing and Management—Bi-monthly

peer reviewed print journal published by Elsevier Science.

14. Information Research: an international electronic journal—Presents research papers and working papers from a variety of information-related disciplines, including information science, information management, information systems, information policy and librarianship.
15. Information Today—Product information and news for librarians.
16. Informing Science: International Journal of an Emerging Discipline—Information systems, library science and journalism evolve to form a new discipline. Quarterly journal available in print or online.
17. International Information and Library Review—Progress and research in international and comparative librarianship, documentation, and information retrieval. Published quarterly by Academic Press.
18. International Journal of Information Management—Aimed at "managers charged with the responsibility of designing and managing complex information systems." From Elsevier Science
19. International Journal on Digital Libraries—Quarterly print journal emphasizing digital information and libraries. Register for email notification of contents.
20. Issues in Science & Technology Librarianship— Electronic journal from the Science and Technology Section of the Association of College and Research Libraries.
21. Journal of Digital Contents (JDC)—International quarterly journal about the management, presentation and uses of contents in digital environments.
22. Journal of Digital Information—A peer reviewed e-journal focusing on information in digital environments. Supported by the British Computer Society and Oxford University Press.
23. Journal of Electronic Publishing—Articles with archives about electronic publishing.
24. Journal of the American Society for Information Science (JASIS)—Flagship publication of the American Society for Information Science available online or in print by subscription. Links to tables of contents and brief abstracts from 1992 to present.
25. Law Library Journal—Official journal of the American

Association of Law Libraries. Includes subscription information and links to selected articles from 2000 to the present.

26. Libraries and Culture—A print based journal that explores the significance of libraries; their creation, organization and preservation in the context of cultural and social history.
27. Library and Information Update—Monthly magazine of the Chartered Institute of Library and Information Professionals. Includes selected articles from past issues.
28. Library Hi Tech—A quarterly, peer reviewed, scholarly journal on computing and technology for library scientists. Links to subscription information, submission guidelines and tables of contents for past issues.
29. Library Journal Digital—Library Journal's online edition. Features current news about libraries and librarians. Includes job opportunities.
30. Library Philosophy and Practice—Peer reviewed online journal specializing in applied library science research. Articles available for downloading in PDF form. Links to guidelines for submission.
31. Library Quarterly—Prestigious print journal of scholarly research from The University of Chicago Press. Subscription information, submission guidelines, tables of contents from 1996 to the present and general information.
32. Library Resources & Technical Services—Details about the journal including information on subscribing and submitting articles.
33. LIBRES: Library and Information Science Research Journal—International, peer reviewed, online journal devoted to new research in Library and Information Science.
34. LISNews.com—Blake Carver's online Library and Information Science News Digest. Apropos articles culled from a variety of sources. Links, polls, submission guidelines and email updates.
35. MC Journal: The Journal of Academic Media Librarianship—A peer-reviewed online journal for practical and scholarly information concerning academic media librarianship.

36. The Public-Access Computer Systems Review— Online journal about end-user computer systems in libraries from University of Houston Libraries. Full text available from 1990 to present. Includes author/ subject index and submission guidelines.
37. Russian Digital Libraries Journal - Electronic journal containing information on research and use of digital libraries.
38. Searcher: The Magazine for Database Professionals—Print based journal with 10 issues annually. Tables of contents and some full text available online along with subscription and submission information.
39. Teacher Librarian: The Journal for School Library Professionals—Offers access to selected past articles, reviews of books and software for resource centers, as well as links to online resources.
40. Transactions on Information Systems—The official publication of the Association for Computing Machinery. Available online or in print. Includes links to an extensive digital library and subscription information.
41. The Wired Librarian's Newsletter—Advice on the implementation of microcomputers in libraries. In publication since 1983.

4

List of Some Indian Library Journals & Place of Publications

1. Annals of Lib. & Inf. Studies—NISCAIR, New Delhi
2. Granthalaya—Kolkata
3. Herald of Lib. Science—Lucknow

4. IASLIC Bulletin—Kolkatta
5. ILA Bulletin—New Delhi
6. Index India—Jaipur
7. Indian J of Information, Libraries & Society—Cuttack
8. Indian Journal Of Information Library & Society (I.J.I.L.I.S).—Cuttack
9. Indian Library Science Abstract—Kolkata
10. Indian Library Science Abstract—Kolkata
11. J of Lib. Inf. Science—Chandigarh
12. Library Herald—New Delhi
13. Library Progress—Modinagar
14. Library Science with Slant to Documentation and Information Studies—Bangalore
15. SRELS J. of Inf. Management—Bangalore

5

Major Library Consortia and Organizations in the International Basi

1. ALA—American Libraries Association - http://www.ala.org
2. ARL—Association of Research Libraries - http://www.arl.org
3. IFLA—International Federation of Library Associations - http://www.ifla.org

4. OCLC—Online Computer Library Center, Inc. - Includes the OCLC Libraries list, Participating Institutions List, and OCLC-Affiliated U. S. Regional Networks - http://www.oclc.org
5. RLG—Research Libraries Group - Information and links to its 159 Member Institutions - http://www.rlg.org
6. SLA—Special Libraries Association – http://www.sla.org
7. IASLIC—Indian Association of Special Libraries & Information Centre http://www.iaslic.org
8. ILA—Indian Library Organisation , http://www.ilanet.org
9. SIS—Society for Information Science, http://sis-india.netfirms.com/

6

Library and Information Science Links

Important Web Pages

1. NDIIPP—National Digital Information Infrastructure and Preservation Program-http://www.digitalpreservation.gov/
2. Beta Phi Mu—http://www.beta-phi-mu.org/
3. National Commission on Libraries and Information Science - http://www.nclis.gov/
4. UKOLN Public Library Networking Focus—http://www.ukoln.ac.uk/public/
5. Documents in Information Science—http://dois.mimas.ac.uk/
6. WebJunction—http://www.webjunction.org/
7. LibraryHQ.com—http://www.libraryhq.com/
8. ODLIS: Online Dictionary of Library and Information

Science http://www.wcsu.edu/library/odlis.html

9. Library and Information Science: Finding Resources in this Subject Area http://www.lub.lu.se/netlab/documents/lisres.html
10. The Libraries FAQ—http://www.ibiblio.org/librariesfaq/
11. Library Link—http://www.emeraldinsight.com/librarylink/
12. Library Underground—http://www.libraryunderground.org/
13. Planning and Building Libraries—http://www.slais.ubc.ca/resources/architecture/index3.html
14. Library and Information Studies Resources—http://www.libraries.rutgers.edu/rul/rr_gateway/research_guides/lib_info/lib_info.shtml
15. LibrarySupportStaff.com—http://www.librarysupportstaff.com/
16. Infolibrarian.com—http://www.infolibrarian.com/
17. DREI—Digital Reference Education Initiative - http://drei.syr.edu/qauthority_pub/
18. What is the Future of the Book in the Digital Era?—http://www.honco.net/9809/roundtable.html
19. Iran Library and Information Science—http://www.geocities.com/iranlibrary/
20. Top Technology Trends for Libraries—http://www.ala.org/ala/lita/litaresources/toptechtrends/midwinter2000.htm
21. Librarians' Resource Center—http://www.sla.org/chapter/ctor/toolbox/resource/cover.htm
22. Infography about Library News—http://www.infography.com/content/676024803275.html
23. Library Support Staff Resource Center—http://www.lib.rochester.edu/ssp/default.htm
24. Libr.org—http://libr.org/ Hosts a variety of library and library science related sites.

7

Library Software

Library Softwares: India

Autolib, Easylibsoft, E-Grantalaya, Gynodaya, Libra 2000, Librarian, Library Manager, Libris, Libsuite, Libsys, Bibliosis, Nalanda, NewGenLib, NexLib, SLIM (System for Library Information and Management) , SOUL (Software for University Libraries), SWIRL [Software for Information Retrieval] [Cataloguing]

Library Softwares: International

ADLIB Library for Windows—Most of the library functions can be carried out using this integrated software. Web interface of catalogue is also possible. Demo is available for download.

Alice Library Automation Software

Book Librarian for Windows—This software is useful for small school, club or corporate libraries. Catalogue of books and circulation services can be undertaken by using this software.

CDS/ISIS software–UNESCO

Endeavor Voyager—It is based on ORACLE RDBMS. Most of the library functions including web interface of library catalogue can be undertaken.

EOS Library Systems - Available in two series viz. Q-Series for large libraries and GLASS for medium sized libraries. Both run on Windows Platform.

Keystone Library Automation System 6.1 - At present only circulation, cataloguing, patron service, OPAC and scheduling and media booking modules are available.

Innovative Interfaces Millenium - Millennium is Innovative's next-generation automated library system. It is a Web-based, open-platform system that offers the best and most complete functionality of any library automation software. The Java™ interface offers staff and patrons an intuitive, easy-to-use, and platform-independent system.

MINISIS – It is a multi-platform object-oriented relational database management tool. It has been developed, distributed, and suppoıted since 1975 by The International Development Research Centre.

OLIB 7 - It is an ORACLE based integrated library management system. Most of the library operations can be carried by using this software.

Sagebrush Library Automation systems - Sagebrush offers three top automation systems viz. Accent, Athena and Winnebago Spectrum for integrating information management, catalog searching, and Internet access for libraries of every type and size.

SIRSI Integrated Library Management System - Most of the house keeping operations of library can be undertaken. Different versions are available depending upon type of library viz. Public, Special, Academic etc. Web interface is availabe with Z39.50 technology.

STAR/Libraries - STAR/Libraries is a multi-purpose system for automating libraries and information centers.

Techlib and TLC Integrated Library Systems.

8

Sci-Tech Databases

Web of Science—Provides citations, author abstracts, and cited references (footnotes to a scholarly article) to more than 8,100 peer-reviewed science and social science journals. Dates of coverage, 1985 to present. Corresponds to the Science Citation Index and Social Science Citation Index. Includes the capability to perform a cited reference search, which allows you to find articles from journals that have cited a book, a patent, or another article. Indexes articles, bibliographies, book reviews, editorials, letters, meeting abstracts, notes, review papers, reviews of software, and more. Useful for identifying the important (ranked) Education journals by using the Journal Citations Reports for the Science journals (most recent data on diskette at the Reserves Desk, Jackson Library).

ACM Digital Library—Provides the full text of approximately 300 publications of the Association for Computing Machinery. Covers journals, magazines, transactions, proceedings, newsletters, and publications by affiliated organizations and special interest groups (SIGs). Provides customization and tables of contents services. Also includes the Online Computing Reviews Service (critical reviews of the computing literature).

Agricola—Provides citations on all aspects of agriculture, including agricultural economics, geography, agricultural engineering, home economics, animal science, human nutrition, chemistry, life sciences, energy, natural resources, entomology, plant diseases, cooperative extension, insect pests and their control, food science, rural sociology, forestry, and veterinary medicine.

Includes over 3.5 million citations from 881 sources. Citations refer to journal literature, government reports, patents, audiovisual materials, books, book chapters, computer databases and software, maps, manuscripts, and dissertations acquired by the National Agricultural Library and cooperating institutions.

Aid Search—Provides citations to published research, a dictionary, and data on clinical trials. AIDSearch is a combination of three databases (MEDLINE AIDS/HIV, AIDSDRUGS, and AIDSTRIALS) providing information about Acquired immunodeficiency syndrome (AIDS) and related topics. All three databases are from the National Library of Medicine (NLM). MEDLINE AIDS/HIV is a subset of Medline providing citations from journal articles, government reports, letters, technical reports, meeting abstracts/papers, monographs, special publications, theses, books and audiovisuals covering research, clinical aspects and health policy issues related to AIDS. AIDSDRUGS is a dictionary of chemical and biological agents currently being evaluated in the AIDS clinical trials covered in AIDSTRIALS. AIDSTRIALS includes information about the clinical trials of substances being tested for use against AIDS, HIV infection, and AIDS-related opportunistic diseases.

Basic BIOSIS—Indexes 300 core life science journals. Covers biology and life sciences, environmental sciences, public health, and natural history. Intended for undergraduate non-biology majors.

Biological Abstracts (BIOSIS)—Provides citations and abstracts for over 4,000 biology and life science journals published worldwide. Covers anatomy, biochemistry, biophysics, botany, cell biology, ecology, evolution, genetics, human biology, microbiology, physiology, reproduction and sex, and zoology. List of journals covered For coverage from 1926 to 1968, use the print version of Biological Abstracts at QH301 .B37.

BioOne—Provides the full text of over 60 journals in the biological, ecological, and environmental sciences.

Cinahl—Indexes about 1,200 nursing and allied health journals; full text links are provided for many journals. Covers all aspects of nursing and nursing education, allied health, biomedical, consumer health, and patient education. Books and book chapters, dissertations, standards of practice, and reviews of educational software packages are also indexed.

Clinical Pharmacology—Provides current and clinically-relevant drug monographs for all U.S. prescription drugs, hard-to-find herbal and nutritional supplements, over-the-counter products and new and investigational drugs. Drugs may be searched by their generic or brand names. Clinical Pharmacology includes Drug Monographs and Patient Education Records. Drug Monographs include description, mechanism of action, and pharmacokinetics. Patient Education Records contain such information as what the medication is used for, what their health care professional should know before taking the medication, how the medication should be taken, what they should do if a dose is missed, what other medications can interact, what side effects may be noticed, what to watch for, and where to keep the medication.

Earthscape—An integrated, interdisciplinary resource that connects the Earth and environmental sciences with their social, political, and economic dimensions. Offers links to web sites for conferences, seminars, books and journal articles from around the world. Also includes data sets, teaching activities, teaching resources and current issues discussions. Provides a wide range of resources, many in full-text, in earth science, astronomy and biology.

Although it primarily serves undergraduates, Earthscape is also an online reference for graduate students and professionals

Encyclopedia of Life Sciences—Provides the full text of over 3,000 peer-reviewed articles in the biological sciences. Includes illustrations, tables, figures, references, and source of further reading.

From the publishers of Nature.

GEOBASE—Provides citations and abstracts for journals, books, monographs, conference proceedings, and reports on geography, geology, and ecology. Core areas include cartography, climatology, energy, environment, geomorphology, hydrology, meteorology, paleontology, photogrammetry, and volcanism.

HealthSource Nursing—Indexing and abstracting for over 1,000 Nursing, Allied Health, and Nutrition periodicals. Full text available for 540 scholarly journals

MathSciNet—Contains more than 1.7 million citations (with abstracts since July 1979) to books, journals and conference proceedings. Covers math, statistics, and computer science, and their applications in mechanics, physics, engineering, operations research, systems theory and control, quality control, and other areas. Indexes over 59 years of Mathematical Reviews and Current Mathematical Publications (from 1940 to the present). Current Mathematical Publications is a subject index of bibliographic data for recent and forthcoming publications. Most items are later reviewed in Mathematical Reviews. All items in Mathematical Reviews appear first in Current Mathematical Publications. Links to some full text sources are provided with subscribetion.

MEDLINE—This databases index articles from leading medical and life sciences journals. Subject coverage includes biology, microbiology, environmental health, nutrition, public health, anatomy, physiology, genetics, sports medicine, and hospital administration plus much more. Citations in these databases are compiled by the National Library of Medicine, the world's largest medical library.

Science Direct—Provides access to full text of over 1,500 scholarly journals from Elsevier. While the primary focus is the natural sciences and medicine, scholarly journals in the humanities and the social sciences are also included. Users can search one, all, or a combination of subjects.

Textile Technology Index—Provides indexing and some full text of hundreds of journals covering textiles and apparel. While the historical emphasis of this index has been technological aspects of textile production and processing, it now also covers marketing and design. Also covers books, conferences, theses, technical reports, and trade literature. Indexes some important books as far back as the 1800's. First published in 1944, as the Institute of Textile Technology's Textile Technology Digest.

9

Indian Discussion Forums, List Service

- LIS-Forum - Discussion forum for library and information professionals in India
  Submissions: lis-forum@ncsi.iisc.ernet.in
  List info: http://ncsi.iisc.ernet.in/mailman/listinfo/lis-forum
- IATLIS - Indian Association for Teachers in Library and Information Science discussion forum
  Submissions: iatlis@yahoogroups.com
  List info: http://groups.yahoo.com/group/iatlis/
- Corporatelibrns An interactive forum for corporate librarians
  Submissions: corporatelibrns@yahoogroups.com
  List info: http://groups.yahoo.com/group/corporatelibrns/
- Digital Libraries: India
  Submissions: digilib_india@yahoogroups.com
  List info: http://groups.yahoo.com/group/digilib_india/
- NMLIS - New Millennium LIS Professionals
  Submissions: nmlis@yahoogroups.com
  List info: http://groups.yahoo.com/group/nmlis/
- INDIA-LIS - The INDIA-LIS is a Library and Information Science in India Mailing List
  Submissions: india-lis@infoserv.inist.fr
  List info: http://infoserv.inist.fr/wwsympa.fcgi/info/india-lis

10

Computer Capacity Measurement

1.	8 Bits	= 1	Byte
2.	1 Byte	= 1	Character
3.	1024 bytes	= 1	KB (Kelo Byte)
4.	1024 KB	= 1	MB (Mega Byte)
5.	1024 MB	= 1	GB (Giga Byte)
6.	1024 GB	= 1	TB (Tera Byte)

11

Library Organisations / Associations

	Year of Estat.	H.Qr.
ALA (American Library association)	1876	Chicago
LA (Library Association, UK)	1877	Landan
SLA (Special Library association, USA)	1909	Washin-gton
IFLA (Intl. Federation of Lib. Association & Institution)	1927	The Hague

COMLA (Commonwealth Library Association)	1972	Kingstan
ASLIB (Association for Information Management)	1924	Landan
CARL (Carlifornia Academic & Research Libraries	1929	Australia
ILA (Indian Library Association)	1933	New Delhi
IASLIC (Ind. Association of Special Libraries & Inf. Centres)	1955	Calcutta
SIS (Society for Information Science)	1975	NewDelhi
GILA(Government of Indian Library Association)	1955	NewDelhi
IATLIS(Ind. Association of Teachers of Lib. & Inf. Science)	1969	New Delhi
SALIS (Society for Advancement of Library and Inf. Science)	1945	Chennai

12

World and Their Origin

Word	*Original Word*	*Original Language*
Catalogue	Keta+Logos	Greek
Classification	Classic	Latin
Census	Censer	Latin
Index	Indicare	Latin
Information	info (Generic Word)	Greek
Dictionary	Dictionarium	Latin
History	Histona	Latin
Glossary	Glossorium	Latin
Vocabulary	Vocubularium	Latin
Encyclopadia	Encyklios	Greek
Communication	Communis	Latin
Thesaurus	(Synonym)	Greek
Bibliography	(Book)	Greek
Education	Educantum	Latin

13

Library and Information Science Job Listing

Following links provide details about the jobs available in India and abroad. Please go through the links provided on each of them for further details. Search can be done by entering keyword as Library in the search box.

India

- ❑ http://www.thehindu.com/Recruitment
- ❑ http://www.Naukari.com
- ❑ http://www.Timesjobs.com
- ❑ http://www.infolibrarian.com
- ❑ http://www.indiainfo.com
- ❑ http://www.creerindia.com

International

- ❑ http://www.monster.com/
- ❑ http://www.freepint.com
- ❑ http://www.cilip.org
- ❑ http://www.Lisjobnet.com
- ❑ http://www.Libjobs.com
- ❑ http://www.LISjobs.com
- ❑ http://www.Ipl.org
- ❑ http://www.Lita.org
- ❑ http://www.Lisjobpostings.org

14

Origin of Library Schemes of Classifications

1.	DDC (Dewey Decimal Classification) by Melville Dewey, England	1876
2.	UDC (Universal Decimal Classification) by Paul Otlet & Henri La Fontaine	1905
3.	CC (Colon Classification) by SR Ranganathan 1933& Henri La Fontaine	
4.	LCC (Library of Congress Classification) Library of Congress	1904
5.	BC (Bibliographical Classification)	1935
6.	SC (Subject Classification)	1906
7.	RIC (Riders International Classification)	1961
8.	BSO (Broad System of Ordering) by UNISIST	1978
9.	Bliss Classification Schemes by Henry Evelyn Bliss	1902
10.	Expansive Classification	1891

15

Universal Decimal Classification

Universal Decimal Classification Consortium home page http://www.udcc.org/

UDC Complete Edition. Derived from the Master Reference File (MRF) from the UDC Consortium, it contains over 65,000 entries and comes in two volumes: V1(All Tables) & V2 (Indexs). (1993 is prepared on the basis of MRF) 1993-MRF (Master Reference File) database, IME (Intl. Medium Edn): English Text Ed.2 (BS: 1000M, 2 Part), BSI order ref BIP 0017-1 Price £175*. It is developed by Paul Otlet and Henri la Fontaine at the end of the 19th century. It is based on the Dewey decimal classification, but is much more powerful. It uses auxiliary signs to indicate various special aspects of a subject and relationships between subjects. It thus contains a significant faceted or analytic-synthetic element, and is used especially in specialist libraries. UDC has been modified and extended over many years to cope with the increasing output in all disciplines of human knowledge.

Main Classes and Notation

0=Generalities	UDC Complete Edition. Derived from the Master Reference File (MRF)
1=Philosophy	Volume 1 – Systematic Tables: All 10 Tables +Auxiliary Tables Summary
2=Religion	Volume 2 – Alphabetical Index: Access to Tables+Conjuction to Volume I
3=Social Science	Notation
4=Philosophy	. Full stop
5=Natural Sciences	+ Plus Addition e.g. 59+636 Zoology and animal

	breeding
6=Applied Science	/ Stroke Extension e.g. 592/599 everything from 592 to 599 inclusive
7=Arts	: Colon Relation e.g. 17:7 Relation of ethics to art
8=Literature	[ ] Square Sign e.g. 31:[622+669](485)statistics of mining and metallurgy
9=Geography	= Equal Sign e.g. = 20 in English; 59=20 Zoology, in English

UDC: For Quick References

1. Aesthetics -18
2. Agriculture - 63
3. Ancient History - 93
4. Architecture - 72
5. Astronomy -52
6. Bibliography - 01
7. Biography - 92
8. Biological Sciences -57
9. Botany -58
10. Building Industry - 69
11. Chemical Technology - 66
12. Chemistry -54
13. Christian theology – 22/28
14. Commerce/Trade Transport-38
15. Devl. of Language -40
16. Drawings - 74
17. Economics -33
18. Education -37
19. Encyclopedias - 03
20. Engineering - 62
21. Engraving & Pints – 76
22. Entertainment - 79
23. Ethics -17
24. Ethnography- 39
25. Geography - 91
26. Geology -55
27. Historyof Philosophy- 19
28. Home Sciences - 64
29. Individual Literatures – 82/89

30. Industries - 67
31. Journalism - 07
32. Law - 34
33. Library Science - 02
34. Logic- 16
35. Management - 65
36. Manuscripts -09
37. Mathematics -51
38. Medical Sciences - 61
39. Metaphysics -12
40. Modern History – 94/99
41. Music - 78
42. Natural Theology – 21
43. Non-Christian religion - 29
44. Painting- 75
45. Paleontology - 56
46. Periodicals- 05
47. Philosophical Systems - 14
48. Photography - 77
49. Physical Planning -71
50. Physics -53
51. Politics -32
52. Polygraph -08
53. Psychology -15
54. Public Administration - 35
55. Sculpture - 73
56. Social Welfare -36
57. Sociology - 30
58. Special Trades - 68
59. Statistics -31
60. Structural of Language – 41
61. Zoology - 59